2070

NUFFIELD
ECONOMICS
&BUSINESS

CO-EDUCATIONAL DIVISION

Competition and Control
Who has power in the market?

LONGMAN

Copyright acknowledgements

The Nuffield Economics and Business Project team and the Publishers are grateful to the following for permission to reproduce copyright material:

Confederation of British Industry for an adapted extract from *Report of the Manufacturing Advisory Group 1991*; Economist Newspapers for adapted extracts from articles in *The Economist* 20.11.93, 12.3.94, 19.3.94; Incomes Data Services Ltd for an extract from *IDS Pay Directory*; Guardian Newspapers Ltd for an abridged extract from the article 'Video rivals seek format accord' in the *Guardian* 16.2.93, F. T. Business Enterprises Ltd for extracts from articles in the *Financial Times* 1.12.92, 17.2.94, 17.3.94, 11.4.94, 15.4.94, 19.4.94; Newspaper Publishing plc for an adapted extract from the article 'Peace, love and ice cream' in the *Independent on Sunday* 3.4.94; Observer Newspapers Ltd for an adapted extract from the article 'CD pricing in dire straits' in *The Observer* 11.4.93; Reed Business Publishing Group Ltd for an adapted extract from the article 'In search of quality' in *Accounting Technician* March 1993; Times Newspapers Ltd for the article 'Sainsbury lures with a new line: media' in *The Times* 4.8.93 © Times Newspapers Ltd 1993.

Thanks are also due to the following for permission to reproduce figures:

British Standards Institute for Figure 2.2; Campaign for Real Ale for Enquiry 3 opening evidence; Central Statistical Office for Figures 4.4, 4.5, Enquiry 2 opening evidence, Enquiry 5 opening evidence; Department of Transport for Figure 3.5; The Economist for Figures 2.4, 3.5 and 3.6; Employment Gazette for Figure 4.7; Environmental Council for Figure 3.3; Financial Times for Figure 4.3; Friends of the Earth for Figure 3.6; The Guardian for Figure 3.4; Macmillan Publishers for Figure 1.7; OECD for Figures 4.11, 4.12.

Acknowledgement is also due to the following for permission to reproduce illustrations on the pages indicated:

The Economist for pp. 74 and 86; Dylan Garcia and Pano Pictures for p. 29; Popperfoto for pp. 35 and 85; Rex Features for p. 72; Squib for p. 92.

Longman Group Limited
Longman House, Burnt Mill,
Harlow, Essex, CM20 2JE, England
and Associated Companies throughout
the world.

© The Nuffield Foundation 1995

ISBN 0 582 24582 6

First published 1995

Designed and typeset by
Ken Vail Graphic Design, Cambridge

Printed in Singapore by Longman
Singapore Publishers Pte Ltd

The Publisher's policy is to use paper
manufactured from sustainable forests.

Contents

About this book

The resources that have been developed by the Nuffield Economics and Business Project are designed specifically to support the Nuffield A levels in Economics and Business. These courses are examined by London Examinations. Although written for a particular course, this book may be found useful by anyone who is studying A level Economics or Business Studies, or who is interested in the subject matter.

This book is one of a series of six designed to support the course options. It covers Option 4, and in combination with any one of the other five options, leads to a joint A level in Economics and Business.

The book is intended to underpin about 10 weeks' work in the later stages of the A level course. It assumes that the reader has a working knowledge of basic economic theory and fundamental business concepts. It assumes an understanding of the nature of competition, oligopoly and monopoly and of supply and demand and elasticities. Some knowledge of marketing strategies, including pricing, is also assumed and of employer–employee relationships and corporate culture. An understanding of the phases of the business cycle will also be helpful. The book can be read in conjunction with any introductory economics or business text but fits neatly alongside the *Student's Book* written for the Nuffield Project.

Nuffield Economics and Business courses require students to investigate themes and issues in order to achieve an understanding of the subject matter. So the book is structured around five Enquiries. Each Enquiry opens with a range of related questions. Some guidance on how to pursue the Enquiries is provided in the Enquiry Guide that follows.

In reading this book, it is important to remember that you are being given a source of information, rather than an all-embracing analysis of markets. How you use this information is up to you. It is therefore essential that you form your own ideas, explore and develop them and apply what you already know in order to analyse the situations described.

A section of this book is about government policies. It is therefore unavoidable that it will date, as policies change. You should seek to find out what changes have taken place since it was written and evaluate the effect of the changes. In particular, referrals under the competition laws are going on all the time, and reports of recent ones will provide illuminating comparisons.

In this book, the term European Community or EC is used where events up to the end of 1993 are under discussion. For subsequent events, the institution is referred to as the European Union or EU.

Ideally, you should find that your enquiries do not stop when you finish this book, but become a basis for further thought and for a continuing watch on competitive forces and market power in the future.

Enquiry guide

Each of the five Enquiries in this book is intended to take about two weeks of subject time. The precise nature of the Enquiry is to be determined by you, the reader. You will need to consult a variety of sources: other books, databases, newspapers and periodicals. If you have access to IT databases and to CD-ROM you will find these helpful.

The questions

Each Enquiry opens with questions, presented in diagrammatic form so that the links between them are made as clear as possible.

These questions highlight important issues and perspectives which can be investigated during the Enquiry. They are not exhaustive in scope and they tend to be rather general. You will need to break them down into subsidiary questions, which you should arrange in a logical order. You should then create a hierarchy of questions and ask yourself:

■ How are these questions related to each other?
■ Which questions are the most important?
■ Can they be answered with the information available?
■ What other information will be needed in order to illuminate the issues?

The opening evidence

The opening evidence presents a range of quotations, public statements, case studies, data and so on. Different points of view are put forward and the data cover a number of the angles which will need to be considered. Again, the opening evidence is not exhaustive: further data appear in the text and the reader who pursues the Enquiry diligently will find much other relevant data elsewhere.

The opening evidence will help you to get started on your investigation and to get a feel for the difficult issues which are a part of your enquiry. It should raise questions in your mind which will become the main focus of your enquiry.

The text

The text forms the main body of this book and underpins the Enquiry. It does not, for the most part, provide answers to the questions. But it does present a good deal of information which can be *used* to answer the questions. You should take your knowledge of economics and business and apply it to the evidence. The text and all the other sources you can find will help you to arrive at an understanding of the issues identified. Then you will be able to develop your own analyses of market situations.

In the margins, beside the text, there are references to various economic and business concepts. You will need to use these ideas in order to understand fully the situations described.

Also in the margins you will find 'Open Questions'. These are questions that do not have a simple answer, but which should be considered carefully. They relate to issues upon which no agreement can necessarily be expected, but which it is important to discuss.

The outcome of your enquiry will be an analysis of the issues you have explored.

Acknowledgements

The development of the courses and resources of the Nuffield Economics and Business Project has been undertaken primarily by the Project Co-Directors: Stephen Barnes, David Lines, Jenny Wales and Nancy Wall. The Project team devised the approach used in all the Option books.

This book was written by Keith Brumfitt, with a substantial contribution from Nancy Wall, who is also editor of the Project publications. John Dymott, David Whitehead and Roy Wilkinson read the first draft and commented, for which the Project team are most grateful. Ian Marcouse and Stephen Barnes read, commented, read again and contributed at all stages of writing. We are very much indebted to them for their help.

The help and support of the Project's administrator, Linda Westgarth, whose contributions were so many and so great that they cannot be briefly described, were essential to both the development work and the final preparation of the book for publication.

NANCY WALL
Editor

Acknowledgements

Enquiry 1: What is market power?

Scope

Market power needs to be considered from three viewpoints. First, there is the theory, which helps to explain how and why market power develops. Then there is the overview of market power in the economy as a whole, which shows which groups of people have market power. Lastly, it is possible to apply this thinking to the situation of a business or of an individual. Each firm, each product and each person have their own particular circumstances. This Enquiry considers some of the sources of market power and the conditions which determine the nature of market power. It concentrates primarily on market power as it applies to an individual business or product; the subject of market power and the individual person is dealt with in subsequent Enquiries.

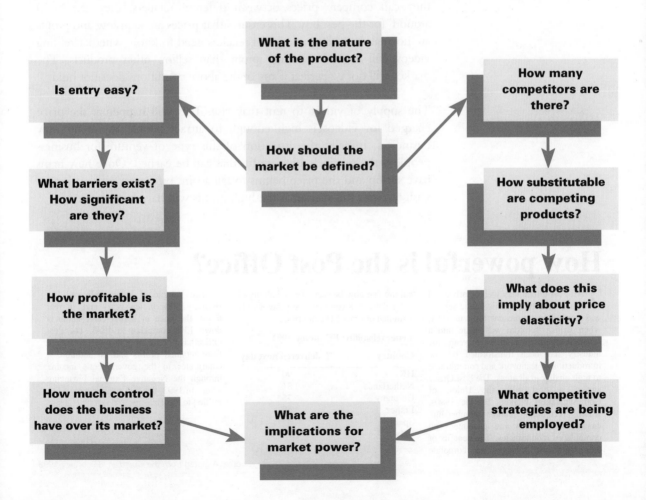

Opening evidence

Video rental shops

Video rental shops in large towns may be thought to operate in an almost perfectly competitive market. The reasons advanced for this assumption are:

■ The videos for hire are identical in all the shops.
■ There are many shops renting out the videos.
■ There are a lot of customers wishing to rent videos.
■ Customers can easily make comparisons between retailers and have a great deal of information about the product and the sellers.
■ It is relatively cheap to set up a new shop for renting out videos; a retailer can simply add a new section to an existing shop display.

If consumers know the price each shop charges for renting videos and they can compare prices between different retailers, they can 'shop around' for the best buy. This ensures that prices are kept low and profits are normal. In addition potential retailers need to know whether renting videos will earn them more profit than selling other products. The market will not be perfect if any of the above conditions does not hold.

The supply of videos to rent may rise. This will happen if the price charged for videos is high enough to attract people to set up new businesses. Initially, the attraction of this type of venture for business people is the relatively high profits that can be earned. Once new firms have set up and the price begins to fall again, businesses will no longer wish to enter this market as the high profits will have been eroded.

How powerful is the Post Office?

THE Post Office may well be privatised in the near future. This public service was created in its present form in 1981, when British Telecom was made into a separate organisation. In recent years, the industry has been transformed by the introduction of teamwork and commitment to high quality in all areas. The Post Office agreed a deal with the Union of Communication Workers for the 1990s, which recognises union membership, ensures consultation and guarantees no compulsory redundancies. The benefits of these dramatic changes in corporate culture can now be seen. The reliability of letter deliveries compares very favourably with that of other EU countries.

Letter reliability: EC survey, 1992

Country	% delivered next day
UK	90
Netherlands	81
Germany	75
France	69
Spain	37
Italy	14

The volume of letters delivered has risen by 50% in ten years and, in real terms, the price of a first class stamp is down 13% compared to 1983. The Post Office has to fund all of its own investment from retained profits and, in addition, it contributes to the government's income through the Negative External Financing Limit. In 1993, this will mean paying £181 million to the Treasury.

Source: Adapted from the *Guardian*, 6 February 1993

The cost of lunch

IN July 1993 the Consumers' Association reported that a lunch of Big Mac, coke and chocolate costs less in the UK than in France, but even less in the US than in the UK.

	France (£)	UK (£)	USA (£)
Big Mac	2.22	1.79	1.22
Can of coke	0.96	0.40	0.33
M&Ms	0.60	0.24	0.33
Total	£3.78	£2.43	£1.88

Exchange rates distort the figures slightly but do not account for all the differences. A spokesperson for McDonald's explained: 'We charge what we believe the market will sustain, bearing in mind the competition we face.' From Mars, the owners of M&Ms, a spokesperson commented: 'We charge higher prices where our volumes are low, as they are in France, but we are always hoping to raise volumes by lowering prices.'

Source: Adapted from the *Guardian*, 8 July 1993

Branded failures!

WITH the decline in importance of branded goods, some retailers are able to build up their own-label products. The following figures give the market share of own-label products for the UK.

Product	Share of market of private label
Wine	75
Cheese	65
Prepared chicken meals	63
Fruit juice	60
Canned vegetables	50
Bakery	46
Fish (frozen and other)	46

Source: Adapted from the *Guardian*, 10 August 1993

Price wars

During the summer of 1993 *The Sun* and *Daily Mirror* newspapers engaged in a price war to increase their circulation. *The Sun* slashed its prices to 7p below the price of the *Mirror*. This price war was not just happening among the tabloid newspapers, because *The Times* was reduced in price to 30p (from 45p) during August 1993. Both *The Sun* and *The Times* are owned by the same proprietor, Rupert Murdoch, who also owns other news outlets throughout the world. The end result of this may well be that one of the newspapers will be unable to survive.

A year later, the *Observer* reported that, collectively, the newspapers had lost £109 million in revenues. The biggest loser is alleged to be Murdoch's News International, but the *Mirror* and *The Independent* appear to be facing the most serious threat.

1 Market types

All businesses and all individuals operate within markets. This book analyses the nature of those markets and the balance of power within them. The degree of market power which an individual or a business can command will vary hugely depending on circumstances in the market concerned. In order to assess the extent of market power in each instance, a real understanding of those circumstances is needed.

Market power describes the extent to which a buyer or a seller can influence the price of what is being sold. Alternatively, the quantity of a product coming on to the market may be controlled, rather than the price; or the nature of the product may be influenced. There are usually two important factors which determine market power. One is the nature and degree of competition in the market, and the other is the degree of scarcity of the product.

Market power gives a person, a business or an institution the capacity to determine outcomes in the market place. An exceptionally able manager can command a high income because exceptional ability is scarce. A business which faces little competition can charge more for its product. By claiming that its flavour is unique, Coca-Cola manages to command a consistently higher price than its imitators.

Markets are usually defined as a means by which buyers and sellers can exchange goods or services. Markets are experienced by all sectors of the community. For example:

- A business sells goods or services to individuals, to other firms or to the government.
- The consumer faces a market in purchasing goods and services.
- An employer operates in a market when seeking workers.
- An employee faces a market in finding a job.
- The financier operates in the money market.

Perfect competition

Some markets

Tomato growers do not have much market power. There are many of them in the UK and they all face extremely stiff competition from each other and from the Dutch growers. This is, for practical purposes, perfect competition.

Car manufacturers are in a different situation. Their products are strongly differentiated. Individual product features may have a powerful effect as selling points. They can position their models carefully in the market in order to try to capture particular types of

Imperfect competition

customer. The prices they charge will depend on a careful comparison of what their competitors are charging for similar models. They have a considerable degree of market power in that they can influence both the nature of the product and the price they charge. However this power is greatly constrained by competition with the other car manufacturers.

Diamond merchants De Beers are different again. They have, on the whole, succeeded in controlling the supply of diamonds. They can limit the supply to some degree, thus ensuring that scarcity is maintained.

The spectrum of competition

All businesses operate within their own market circumstances; most are facing competition from other suppliers. Businesses in a situation of strong competition behave very differently from those with few competitors. The behaviour of an independent newsagent is typical of a business facing a great deal of competition. Channel 4 television, on the other hand, has some power and influence in its market.

One way of comparing businesses is according to the number of competitors faced by an individual organisation. Often, it turns out that firms with a similar number of competitors use similar strategies even though their products and services are very different.

Product differentiation

Another highly significant factor determining the way businesses behave is the *directness* of the competition. For example there are many producers of jeans. Even so, Levi occupies a commanding position in the market because of the reputation of its jeans.

Where an industry is dominated by a few large firms, it is described as an **oligopoly**. In an oligopoly, each business is dependent on the actions of the others. This interdependence is an important characteristic of the oligopoly market. Examples of oligopolies range from banking to hotels in a small town. Many manufactured goods have markets with an oligopolistic structure. An important feature of oligopoly is that there are barriers to entry: the minimum efficient scale may be very large, as is the case in the car industry. This ensures that there will be relatively few oligopolistic producers with a considerable degree of market power.

Two other types of market structure will be familiar: **monopoly** and **perfect competition**. A business is in a monopoly situation when it is the only firm in its particular industry and the entry of new firms is impossible, as with British Gas, in relation to domestic consumers. Yet, although these industries have a monopoly in the supply of their service, consumers do have some choice. They do not have to use gas; electricity provides an alternative source of energy, allowing for some competition. Some organisations, such as the water companies, do have local monopolies because consumers have no choice but to buy their product.

The model of perfect competition is a theoretical one but it can provide a useful tool of analysis. In a perfectly competitive market the organisation is one of many selling or producing an identical, homogeneous product. New firms can start up and there should be full information as to what possibilities are available to the consumer and producer. Examples of perfect competition could be growers of horticultural products such as tomatoes, where the products are indistinguishable and consumers do not have any loyalty to one grower's produce.

Normal profit
The opportunity cost of capital

Competition keeps prices low, which is good for consumers. However, prices will not become too low as firms would go out of business if they did not earn enough profit to provide a competitive return on capital invested.

The more monopoly power a business has, the higher is the likely level of super-normal profit, i.e. profit in excess of that needed to keep the resources in the industry. In a perfectly competitive market, super-normal profit will be competed away as firms expand to meet the demand and prices drop to the point where profit is just enough to keep them in business.

Competition among the many

Monopoly and perfect competition are the extreme ends of the spectrum of competition. Oligopoly represents a situation of competition between a relatively small number of firms. **Monopolistic competition** is the term used to describe a different market situation, one in which there are many producers and there is strong competition between them, but they sell differentiated products. Entry to the industry is easy. A firm which wishes to start up can do so without encountering major difficulties.

Free entry

Estate agents

There are many estate agents. They compete with one another in the high street. They offer similar services but each tries to satisfy customers with a personal approach. Some will try to convince customers of their potential for success by putting SOLD signs on their boards. Others will advertise free valuations to people contemplating selling. In other words, they will attempt to differentiate the product. Entry is easy: anyone with the appropriate qualifications can set up as an estate agent.

Text books

Consider any academic subject. For most courses there will be a large number of texts to choose from. Each one will be different, with its own selling points: colour, illustrations, text layout, and so on. Entry is easy: in recent years a number of small publishers have set up in business, some rapidly growing quite large.

The term monopolistic competition applies to many products in the service sector, where a personal touch may serve to provide the element of differentiation. Restaurants each have their own style, price range and ambience. Entry into the business is easy, there are many of them and competition is strong. Yet their products are easily distinguishable and they will each command customer loyalty from people whose tastes they satisfy particularly well.

In such market conditions, small firms need the consumer to be able to distinguish their output from that of their competitors. It may be possible to identify distinctive product benefits that will command a premium price while adding relatively little, or nothing, to costs.

For businesses involved in providing a service, one of the main ways of creating a difference is in the quality of the service. For example, self-employed painters and decorators, independent shop owners, carpet fitters, and so on, may attempt to give good personal service in order to ensure personal recommendations.

Different markets for different products

Many large businesses operate in a variety of markets and it is therefore not always easy to describe the type of competition that any one business faces. Typically, large businesses which have diversified into many markets will experience different degrees of competition in each of their sub-markets.

Disney

The Disney operation has expanded from its original product, cartoon films, into many new markets. Each of these markets has a different degree of competition. The Disney theme parks in Florida and California have a very well-established position in their market. The Euro Disney theme park in France does not have so much strength within its market, perhaps because there are many other tourist attractions in Europe, or perhaps because of the less attractive climate. This has led to the Euro Disney theme park having to alter its prices and give incentives for visitors to stay at the company's hotels. The costs of getting to Euro Disney have been so high that many UK visitors have found it cheaper to fly to Florida. Thus the Florida operation has preserved its market dominance.

Other Disney products, such as souvenirs, face a very competitive market and here the strategy is to build customer loyalty and identify the Disney product as different and of high quality. It is very difficult to describe the overall market facing the company as the different sectors face differing amounts of competition.

2 How is market power measured?

It is useful to have a way of measuring the degree of power exhibited by a company or group of companies. One of the main indicators of how much power a company has is its market share. A business with a 70% share of the market may behave differently from a business with 25% of the market. It is also important to know how many large competitors the dominant company faces as this may also affect company behaviour.

Figure 1.1 A comparison of two different industries

Group of firms	Industry A % of total industry sales	Industry B % of total industry sales
Largest 3	45	45
Largest 5	58	80
Largest 10	63	100
Largest 50	65	100

Which industry has the greater concentration of power? Clearly, it is Industry B, because it has only ten or fewer firms. Both industries could be described as oligopolies because of the power of the largest firms.

It is not always possible to predict company behaviour just by looking at market share. Many other factors can influence their power. Some of these influences, such as the power of consumers and other interest groups, will be considered in later Enquiries.

Concentration ratios

One measurement of market power uses concentration. The percentage of the market accounted for by a certain number of firms is called the

concentration ratio. In Figure 1.2, in the diagram on the left the largest firm has 25% of market share and the largest three have 65%. This is the three-firm concentration ratio. The largest five have 88%; this is the five-firm concentration ratio. This is very different from the diagram on the right, where the figures are 70%, 84% and 92%, respectively. Useful comparisons can be made between the two markets in this way.

Figure 1.2 Concentration ratios

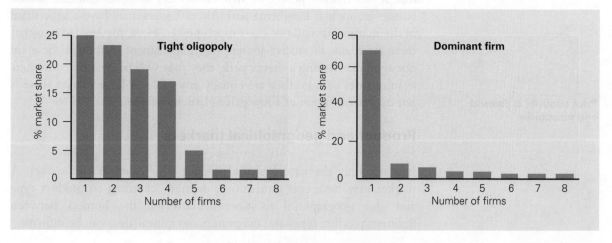

This is only one way of measuring the power of individual businesses, but it does give a very quick and easy way to measure the structure of an industry.

Defining the market

There are many problems with gathering accurate information about how much power one business has. The first of these problems is how to define the market. In order to assess the structure of a market and decide whether there is any abuse of power, it is necessary to determine the boundaries of the market. 'Defining the market' means drawing a circle round all the products that belong in the market and excluding all other products. This is important because determining the size of the market affects the monopoly power that exists within it. For example, the market could be defined as:

1 sources of finance available to a business
2 sources of banking finance available to a business
3 secured sources of banking finance available to a business
4 secured long-term sources of banking finance available to a business.

In the last situation (4), an individual high street bank could exercise considerable power because it seems that any business wishing to borrow money has a very limited range of options. Only the bank could provide such finance. However, using a wider definition, as shown in the first definition (1) above, an individual high street bank's power may seem to be much smaller. The firm could tap a range of alternative sources of finance.

Market share and market power

Just because one company has a large share of the market does not mean that it has market power or that consumers are disadvantaged. Some businesses, such as the theme park Alton Towers, may have a large share of the market but will not exert much power. Here, the key factor is that there are many alternative sources of entertainment. Although these are not at all like visiting a theme park, they may well be seen by consumers as substitutes because they are equally enjoyable. A large market share is not necessarily a sign of a low price elasticity of demand.

Price elasticity of demand and substitutes

Product and geographical markets

It is not only the nature of the product which defines the market. A market may have two dimensions, defined according to product type and also geographical location. Discovering the borders between different product types and different geographical areas can be difficult.

In the market for alcoholic drinks, consumers could buy beer, lager, gin, rum, etc. If these drinks are regarded as substitutes for each other then there is one large market for alcoholic drinks. If they are not considered to be substitutes then there are many separate markets. This approach defines the market according to product type.

The geographical area within which the market exists may be small or large, depending upon the circumstances. A small local shop on a housing estate, miles away from the centre of a town, may well have an effective monopoly in its area. Clearly, some people will travel to other shops in the town centre or to out-of-town shopping centres but many people will be restricted to this one shop because of the cost of travel, the nearness of the shop and the convenience. Effectively, the market in which the shop operates is judged by the number of substitutes available to the potential customers.

A firm which uses mail order distribution may have a geographically large market. The geographical market may, as in this case, be determined by the way the producer chooses to market the product, or it may be determined by the way consumers shop.

Substitutability is the key concept in defining the extent of a market. If two products can be substituted, then they are in the same market. They will be competing with each other. The market power of each will be limited by the existence of the other. The closer the substitutes, the higher their elasticities of demand will be.

A product with no good substitutes faces little competition. It will be in a market of its own and will have considerable market power. The demand for it will be very inelastic with respect to price.

Price elasticity of demand and market power

Elasticity of demand can be influenced by the image of the product. If, through advertising, the company can convincingly present its products as indispensable items, it will reduce the acceptability of alternatives, and will thus give the product a lower price elasticity. Effectively it reduces the threat of competition and narrows the market by weakening the power of competing products. This opens up possibilities: if consumers see the substitute products as inferior, it may be possible to raise the price without sales falling much. As long as price elasticity is less than one, a price increase will raise sales revenue. If it is greater than one, a price increase will mean a proportionately larger fall in quantity demanded and sales revenue will fall. Figure 1.3 shows the two scenarios. When demand is inelastic, the price increase leads to a gain in revenue which is far larger than the lost revenue from the small fall in quantity demanded. When demand is elastic, the fall in quantity demanded leads to a loss of revenue in excess of that gained from the higher price.

Figure 1.3 Price elasticity and potential sales revenue

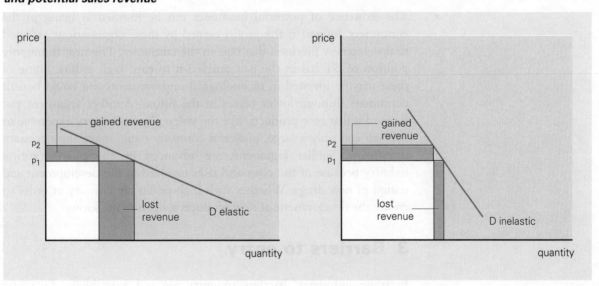

This kind of market power can be created in other ways besides advertising. Suchard mini-Easter eggs appeal to customers with a taste for quality chocolate; the particular selling point of Cadbury's Cream Eggs is

Elasticity and sales revenue

their white and yellow fillings. Both products have a unique appeal. Their brand images allow the makers to charge a relatively higher price because customers with a taste for a particular kind of egg will be prepared to pay more for it. Effectively, both firms have defined a market niche which allows them to charge a higher price and increase added value.

It is important to remember that decisions about what price to charge depend on potential profit as well as on sales revenue. In turn, profit depends partly on cost structures. If, after a price rise, the quantity bought falls, the new lower quantity will have lower direct costs. In deciding on their pricing strategy, firms need to consider the changes in the relationship between revenue and costs which are likely to result from price and quantity changes.

Profitability and power

Businesses which have some power over their prices are generally assumed to be able to earn higher profits. The greater the degree of monopoly power, the lower the price elasticity of demand is likely to be, opening up the possibility that a price increase will lead to rising sales revenue and higher super-normal profit. If there were easy entry to the industry, the resulting profits would attract new entrants and increased competition. However, monopoly power arises precisely because entry is not easy; the existing power of the firms in the industry is likely to continue.

The existence of powerful businesses can be justified as being in the consumers' interest if the profits earned by these organisations are used to develop new products that benefit the consumer. The near monopoly position of BT has in the past enabled it to earn high profits. Some of these may be invested in technological improvements and could benefit consumers through lower prices in the future. Another argument put forward is that new products, like the video phone, are very expensive to develop and only a large, powerful company could make the necessary investment. Similar arguments are advanced by the pharmaceutical industry because of the costs and risks involved in the development and testing of new drugs. Whether such high profits are *necessary* in order to ensure the development of new products is open to question.

3 Barriers to entry

In some industries, barriers to entry are not a problem. Energetic entrepreneurs see a market for their product and start up, often in a small way at first. Many items can be produced on a small scale: design, construction and catering provide examples everywhere. The business can be started using personal savings and bank loans. There may be some risks and uncertainties because of lack of information but these can be overcome by careful planning. This is referred to as easy entry.

Other industries are different. There are **barriers to entry**. Often, this is because there is a high initial cost of entry, caused by the existence of economies of scale. Or patents may be a factor: these allow only the holder of the patent to make the product to which it applies, thus creating a legal monopoly.

Economies of scale

If the minimum efficient scale of production is at a high level of output, there is no possibility of the new entrant starting on a small scale. New businesses will then find it difficult to achieve the low costs of production which established producers can achieve. The standard average total cost curve, which illustrates the existence of economies of scale, shows how this might occur. In Figure 1.4 costs are high for low levels of production and then fall as output rises.

Figure 1.4 New entrants and economies of scale

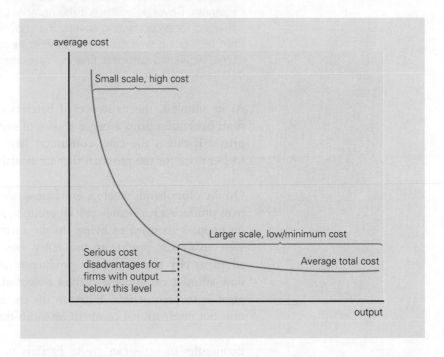

Economies of scale may be technical, financial or managerial. Also, existing large businesses can have advantages over new businesses because they are well known in the market. It can take very large resources to overcome this problem. The types of advantage held by established businesses include greater product awareness among consumers. This can be overcome by advertising but it will add to their costs if they are trying to spread the cost of advertising over a relatively low level of sales. These are referred to as marketing economies of scale.

The launch of Virgin Radio

Having promised the advertisers to deliver 3.3 million listeners per week, Virgin Radio started up on Friday 30 April 1993. The new national station, aimed at the high-spending 20–45-year-olds, plays mainly album tracks with an emphasis on adult oriented rock (AOR). The new station aims to reach about 90% of the population. The station is financed by Virgin Communications (75%) and the investment group Apax (25%). Although there are many local stations playing similar music, the attraction of Virgin Radio is mainly to national advertisers who have limited access to radio. The small independent radio stations are not likely to be hit as hard by Virgin Radio as the large local stations such as Capital and Piccadilly, who rely on large national companies for their income.

There are risks associated with a commercial radio station. Most of the costs are fixed and income is heavily dependent on the number of listeners. Revenue will rise if the number of listeners rises because the charges for broadcasting advertising copy will increase. The risk of this not happening was sufficient to deter new entrants in radio for a long time. Virgin had sufficient financial resources to be able to carry the risk.

At its simplest, the existence of barriers to entry prevents consumers from benefiting from a larger choice of suppliers and consequent lower prices. If this is the case, consumers have less choice and must pay a higher price for the products that are available.

On the other hand, where a few large–scale producers have been able to mass produce a reasonably priced product, they have had a major impact on people's standard of living. In the early years of this century, there were many car producers and entry was easy, yet few people could afford to buy the cars. Mass production means that many people can now afford a car and the market power of car manufacturers is not so great as to prevent this. Entry to the car industry is almost impossible now but international competition limits the effect of the barrier.

Economies of scale can create barriers to entry in the production of cars, aircraft, computer hardware, newspapers, airlines, insurance, and so on. In some industries they are becoming less important as new ways of working and organising business become prevalent. In others, they are likely to remain very significant. However, a powerful conglomerate may have no problem in overcoming high initial costs of entry because it will have financial resources to match the requirements.

Legal barriers

The main legal restrictions faced by businesses are introduced by the government. These can take the form of granting rights to certain organisations and preventing the production of competing products or services. An obvious example is television. Under the 1990 Broadcasting Act, fifteen licences were issued for regional independent television and businesses were encouraged to bid for the rights to broadcast. The conditions imposed by the government involved controls on the ownership of the media, guarantees about regional programmes and a quality threshold. Once these licences were granted, no other businesses could operate an ITV television channel. (Satellite and cable television are outside this control.)

The other important legal barriers come from patents. These protect inventors of new products and processes, making them legally the sole suppliers or users. This gives people an incentive to innovate, guaranteeing that their ideas will not immediately be copied by competitors.

These legal barriers restrict the competition within a market and give existing businesses more power to control their own future. Without the worry of new businesses setting up, established companies are freer to make the most of their situation.

Here again, the impact of patents should not be overestimated. An innovative firm with a strong research team will devise technical strategies of its own. It is not always the case that existing producers have the advantage.

Contestable markets

Entry and exit

Another way of looking at markets is to consider whether they are **contestable**. This means examining how easy it is for businesses both to enter and to exit from a market. If a market is contestable, new businesses can easily set up to take advantage of a perceived opportunity, with the knowledge that they can leave without major extra costs.

Many manufacturing industries do not have easily contestable markets because of the importance of economies of scale. However, small-scale retailing, handicrafts, services such as hairdressing and catering, and many services to business have markets which are likely to be contestable.

A contestable market, where new businesses could set up and leave with relative ease, will be very competitive. The firms that are already in business will take care not to price themselves out of the market. Whether new businesses do set up is not always significant. It is the *possibility* of competition that changes existing business behaviour.

Inside the EU

For a company that operates within a national market in continental Europe, the extra costs involved in selling abroad can be very small. With the introduction of the Single European Market in January 1993, it may well be cheaper to sell abroad rather than in your own home market. A video manufacturer in Lyons would find it cheaper, because of the delivery costs, to sell in Luxembourg and Italy than in Bordeaux. In this way, this video manufacturer can see the Luxembourg and Italian markets as contestable because they are easy to enter, and leave if necessary, and there are no additional costs.

Control over supply

A very important way of controlling the competition is by controlling the supply of raw materials or components. Because the vast majority of computer chips are manufactured by American or Japanese companies (often abroad), these companies can expect to exert influence on any market for goods that use these components, such as televisions, computers, washing machines, etc. By moving along the chain of production, it is possible to influence one market by controlling another.

In some primary product markets there is just one business that has been able to achieve a great deal of control over supply, thus gaining significant market power.

Diamond markets

The majority of diamonds in the world are mined by subsidiaries of the De Beers Corporation or come from the ex-Soviet Union. Until the collapse of communism in Eastern Europe the world market was dominated by De Beers, which, as controller of the sources of raw diamonds, could control the retail side and the whole market. Its approach to this monopolisation was to invite approved dealers to its sales days and to allow only enough diamonds for sale to ensure that prices were maintained. As dealers had no other source of supply, the market was easy to control. No dealer was allowed to stock-pile diamonds or to sell to another dealer, otherwise they would not be invited to subsequent sale days.

Open Question

Is control over supply in the public interest?

4 The use of price as a way of competing

The demand for any product or service is influenced by a large number of factors. If asked, most people would probably answer that price is the single most important factor in deciding what to buy. However, business people know that other factors, such as brand loyalty, image, quality and the level of customers' incomes, are also important. Nevertheless, price remains a very significant consideration in the demand for a company's products.

Very few businesses enjoy the privileged position of a monopoly, either regional or national. The majority of products face an imperfectly competitive market. Some companies rely heavily on price as their main means of competing with rival businesses. The alternative is non-price competition.

There are three main ways in which a business can arrive at a price for its goods or services: based on demand, costs and the level of competition.

Demand-based pricing

When a demand-based pricing strategy is used, decision takers are considering the nature of the market they face and using the strength of consumer demand as the main determinant of the decision, rather than costs of production. This means that once a price has been decided, other decisions, involving costs, follow on. The question is not, how can we cover our costs, but, if we can get this price for the product, can we produce it at a cost which allows us to reach our profit target?

Perceived-value pricing involves finding out from potential customers what they would be prepared to pay for a particular product or product concept.

The *business cycle* may be an important factor in demand-based pricing. In a period when sales are falling, a price increase will make matters worse. When the economy recovers, it may be possible to raise prices without any loss in sales. Rising incomes may make consumers less liable to 'shop around'.

An example of this is the DIY chains which offered discounts and special offers during the recession of the early 1990s. These businesses, such as B&Q, Do-It-All and Homebase, all faced competition from the traditional decorators shop, but the share of the market taken by them steadily increased despite a static market during that period.

The *product life cycle* may dictate pricing strategies. For a product in the early stages of its life cycle it may be that skimming is appropriate. This

Skimming

entails charging a relatively high price because, at this stage, the market will be fairly small but demand will also be relatively inelastic. A high price will not deter the buyers, who will perhaps perceive the product as having high status or interest because of its newness. This will allow the company to earn a quick return on its investment.

Penetration pricing

Later on in the product life cycle, the strategy may change to penetration pricing. The business may deliberately set a low price in order to bring about a substantial increase in market share. The business may want to take an aggressive view of the market and, assuming that price elasticity of demand is high, seek both to expand the market and to take an increasing share of it. An added advantage might be to reap economies of scale through increased sales. If costs fall, prices can be cut at the same time as profits increase. This strategy may also drive competitors out of the market if they are unable to match the new low prices.

There are other demand-based techniques for deciding upon a price:

- Loss leaders – where some items are priced attractively to persuade customers to look at the rest of the products. This is often used in food retailing.
- Known price item (KPI) – where commonly purchased goods are kept at a competitive price to attract customers, whereas goods of which the prices are not well known can be set to earn higher profits. Often used by small retailers, the KPI formula applies to goods such as milk, sugar, coffee and bread, where customers are aware of the supermarket prices and small retailers need to be competitive.
- Psychological pricing is commonly used in retailing where prices are marked at, say, £9.99 or £2.99. The usual reason given is that 'the price is kept below the £10 (or the £3) barrier'. Although it may seem unlikely that consumers are fooled by this, it is an important device for reducing the *perceived* price of a product at minimal cost.

Price discrimination

Price discrimination is a variant of demand-based pricing, based on an assessment of variations in price elasticity of demand in different segments of the market. By charging different prices to different customers, it is possible to increase the company's revenue. British Rail does this, utilising the fact that commuters have a much lower price elasticity of demand than, say, leisure travellers.

Price discrimination only works if the business is able to divide its market into segments and the buyers who are required to pay the higher price can be prevented from buying at a cheaper price. British Rail can do this, for example, by charging according to the time of day. There may be different prices for buying in bulk, prices may vary between the home and export market or mail order prices may differ from the price charged by retailers. Although British Rail no longer exists as a single operator, it seems likely that price discrimination will continue to be used to decide rail fares.

Cost-based pricing

Some businesses will decide their prices purely on the basis of production costs: this is known as *cost-plus pricing*. They will work out the direct cost of producing the actual product and then add a percentage mark-up to cover overheads and profit. For example, if the cost is £40, 25% might be added for gross profit, giving a price of £50. This would cover its overheads and anything remaining would be net profit. This method of pricing can cause problems because the business may not earn enough revenue to cover all its overheads. It depends on whether estimates of both sales and overheads are reasonably accurate. A fall in sales may make it impossible to cover overheads, let alone provide a margin for profit.

Figure 1.5 Overheads and direct costs

Apollo

Apollo cleaning services operates a small home-based carpet cleaning service and is faced with the following costs per month.

Overheads (per month)	(£)	Direct costs (per job)	(£)
Telephonist's wages	600	Driving, etc.	5
Cost of the van	250	Cleaning materials	5
Insurance	50	Labour costs	40
Equipment payments	150	Total	50
Total	1,050		

The cleaning service expects to be employed on three occasions per day for 25 working days in each month. The charge for an average cleaning job would need to be:

$$£50 \text{ (direct costs)} + \frac{1,050 \text{ (indirect costs)}}{75 \text{ (jobs)}} = £64$$

If the business wanted a profit margin of 10% on each cleaning job, then it should charge:

$$£64 \times \frac{100}{90} = £71.11 \text{ (say, £71)}$$

Then suppose that Apollo found it was only getting bookings for two jobs per day. The *contribution* to overheads and profit falls from:

75 × £21 = £1,575, to 50 × £21 = £1,050

A 33% fall in sales has led to a 100% fall in profits. Clearly, any further fall in the number of cleaning jobs will lead to losses.

Cost-plus pricing is sometimes used for large construction projects where changing specifications can lead to uncertainty as to what the final price should be. The buyer agrees to pay the direct costs plus a percentage.

An alternative cost-based approach is to use *full-cost pricing*. This is sometimes called mark-up or average cost pricing. Here, a percentage profit mark-up is added to the total cost of one unit. The total cost must include both direct and indirect costs. Here again, the success of the strategy depends on an accurate calculation of indirect costs.

Target return pricing starts from the other end. It sets a target rate of return on capital investment and sets prices so that this is achieved. Again, overheads must be accurately forecast.

Marginal cost pricing and contribution

Marginal cost pricing may be used if there is spare production capacity which could be used if increased sales were to be achieved. If the price covers direct or marginal costs and makes a contribution to overheads, then it is worth producing and making the sale.

The example of Apollo shows the implications of not getting enough business. If the business fails to reach its target output, the income earned may be insufficient to cover the total costs, let alone reach the target rate of profit. If the business is able to sell more than its planned output then profits will rise very quickly because the overheads have already been covered. Once the overheads have been paid, a business may wish to use a different pricing method.

Competition-based pricing

A business may carefully consider the prices charged by its competitors and decide to base its own price on these figures. It might decide to undercut its competitors or, if it considers its product is better, then the business could set prices higher than the competitors' prices.

BT, Mercury and the cable companies

When Mercury began to offer an alternative to BT for long-distance calls, it advertised the fact that it would offer savings over BT prices. Its pricing decision had little to do with cost or demand-based calculations. It aimed to secure a share of BT's market by charging less.

As people switched to Mercury, BT was forced to reconsider its pricing policies. It cut the weekend rates for long-distance calls and abolished its morning peak rate. Mercury then followed suit. Competition-based pricing is visible in the cable companies' strategies, too. Some of these compete on price; others by offering a better service at a similar price.

Competition-based pricing can usually be observed whenever a new supplier comes into a market place where, previously, there were sellers with some monopoly power. For example, petrol stations in remote areas often charge a high price. A new one may open up nearby and set its prices lower in order to capture a slice of the market.

How competition-based pricing works depends heavily on the nature of the market and the power of the individual business within that market. In a highly competitive market, where all producers are marketing a similar product, the company will be fully aware that a high price will end in very low sales. This situation is close to perfect competition. The producer faces a highly elastic demand and has little choice but to adopt a *going-rate pricing* strategy. Competition will ensure that the price is the lowest that is realistically possible.

Where there are fewer producers or a highly differentiated product, as with an oligopoly, the situation is different. The business will observe its competitors' strategies and decide how to react. It will also try to predict what sort of response it will get to its own pricing policy. Some businesses will seek to protect their own market and some form of retaliation can be expected, while others may not be so keen to compete. There will be a need to consider the percentage of the rival company's profits associated with the product, whether the market is growing and potential profit margins.

If the competing company has a high level of commitment to the product in question, it will respond aggressively to any price changes.

Some oligopolies develop a stable price structure, which reflects their disinclination to compete on price, e.g. CDs are priced higher in the UK than in the USA. Despite a long campaign by W H Smith and the Consumers' Association, CD manufacturers have been able to maintain this position for some time.

CD pricing in dire straits

IN 1992 the Office of Fair Trading looked at the pricing structure of the record industry and concluded that the industry did not make excessive profits. In April 1993 the record industry defended itself against charges of profiteering. Retailers and some musicians called for more moderate pricing, while the UK record industry resisted the claim.

The record industry is dominated by seven companies – Warner, Sony, EMI, Virgin, BMG, Polygram and MCA – who have approximately 80% of the market. The record industry argues that the 10% profit margin within which they operate is not excessive. The cost of manufacturing a CD is around 70p. The record industry sells the CDs to the retailer at a dealer price of between £7.60 and £8.14. For each CD sold, the record industry claims that about £1.50 is paid to the artist. A further 30% of the price is re-invested in A&R (the artists and repertoire department responsible for finding and developing new talent). Recording, marketing and packaging costs are added on top and the net profit taken from each sale is less than £1.

How CDs have conquered (% share of the market)

Year	Cassette	Record	Compact disc
1987	51.4	36.0	12.5
1988	50.5	31.3	18.2
1989	51.1	23.3	25.7
1990	49.8	16.4	33.8
1991	45.3	10.1	44.7

The managing director of WH Smith, which stocks CDs and cassettes and also owns Our Price and 50% of the Virgin Megastore chain, has called for a cut of £2 in the price of CDs. Some people think the high price of CDs is to blame for the 10% decline in the sales of recorded music since 1987. 'The point is that CDs are approaching a price where we can detect consumer resistance,' says Nigel Kenyon Jones, WH Smith's general manager for music, video and computer games. 'We are discounting new CDs to get customers into the stores. We think it would be in everyone's interest if there was a more equitable sharing of the discount between retailers and the record industry.' Ironically, WH Smith stopped selling LPs in 1992 'because there was a steep fall-off in demand for them'.

Source: Adapted from the *Observer*, 11 April 1993

Price leadership is one possible outcome of competition-based pricing when there are relatively few producers. A company that is particularly powerful in the market may decide on a price. All the competing companies will then charge a similar price. If they try to charge more, they will be likely to lose market share. Charging less may precipitate a price war as all the players in the market attempt to recapture their market share. A price war can have a detrimental effect on all of them, reducing profits to a serious degree. The most vulnerable may end up going out of business. A powerful company may, in fact, deliberately cut prices with this outcome in mind: it will be the one to survive and, with fewer competitors, its market power will be enhanced. This is predatory pricing and is examined in Enquiry 2.

If price cutting becomes competitive and a price war results, everyone will lose profits with no advantage in increased market share. Some industries are more vulnerable to price wars than others.

Holiday price wars

One of the industries well known for using price as a basis for competition is the travel industry. Almost every year, one of the large package holiday companies introduces a price cut to attract new customers. In 1993 it was Thomas Cook which got the ball rolling. In August 1993 it announced a 10% discount for early booking of a 1994 holiday. This was immediately followed by Pickfords Travel and Hogg Robinson offering a similar discount. Not to be left out, Airtours offered 100,000 free places for children up to the age of 19! Cosmos offered £7 million worth of free places for people booking early. To some extent it appears that this price war was part of the standard marketing strategy of the holiday companies and a very effective way of getting publicity.

Consumers may benefit from a price war, although this may be temporary. The larger companies will benefit if a smaller company is driven out of the market. Prices may then rise.

Going downmarket

In introducing a different version of an existing product, at a slightly lower price, a business may aim to attract a whole new market segment. However, it also runs the risk of the existing customers moving to the cheaper product with no advantage for the business. Car manufacturers who produce a large range of models have often faced this particular problem. They seek to maintain a hold in different segments of the car market so that customers will not trade down.

Haute couture

Designer fashion wear is all about exclusivity and high prices. Unfortunately, there is not a large market for these goods, even world-wide. For designers to earn money from their clothes, it is essential to be able to sell their goods in a variety of market segments. The clothes you see on display on the catwalks of Milan and Paris will not be available in high street shops and the designers may sell as few as ten copies of each outfit. They make their money by having a cheaper range that sells in expensive boutiques (although still not in the high street shops). A good example of this is American designer Donna Karan, a regular favourite at clothes shows and often reviewed in magazines such as *Cosmopolitan* and *Company*. Her 'cheaper' range of clothes, marketed under the label DKNY (Donna Karan New York) earns the money; the haute couture catwalks create the image.

Few businesses have the luxury of deciding their own prices without considering their competitors' actions. Consequently, businesses will look at other ways of competing as well as adjusting their prices. Price is only one factor in the marketing mix and it would be naïve for any company to rely solely on this one method of improving its profit figures, especially if the outcome is likely to be a price war. The decision of how much emphasis to place on price competition is partly determined by the industry's history but it is also influenced by the nature of the product and the extent of customer loyalty. Many businesses, such as building societies, rely more on non-price competition. Typically the marketing mix includes a range of strategies, including pricing, but with many other features. This is taken up in Enquiry 2.

5 Power, performance and success

Figure 1.7 Generic strategies

Competitive advantage

		Competitive advantage	
		Lower cost	*Differentiation*
Competitive scope	Broad target	Cost leadership	Differentiation
	Narrow target	Cost focus	Focused differentiation

Source: M. Porter, *The Competitive Advantage of Nations,* Macmillan, 1990

Michael Porter looked at different strategies that can be used by the same industry in different countries to improve its performance. The four *generic strategies* shown in Figure 1.7 can be used to explain how some businesses operate. He used the shipbuilding industry to demonstrate the principles:

1 Japanese firms offer a wide variety of high quality ships at premium prices (differentiation strategy).
2 Korean firms offer lower quality, cheaper ships (cost leadership).
3 Scandinavian shipyards specialise in ice breakers and other ships which command high prices to offset high labour costs (focused differentiation).

4 Chinese shipyards, the newly emerging competitors, produce simple, standardised ships at very low cost (cost focus).

Each strategy works in its own setting but it is important to *have* a strategy. Being stuck in the middle or trying to do everything will not be successful. The British shipbuilding industry was not clearly identified with a generic strategy. It could not compete against the Koreans and did not have a specialised sector of the market. As a consequence, it could not compete on the world stage and relied on captive government orders.

The case study above shows how a strategy or a focus can give a firm a competitive advantage in the market place.

Does a business with a competitive advantage also have market power? Michael Porter has explored the way in which strong competition creates competitive advantage. Firms which face a very competitive market have to strive for excellence. They must identify every possible way of improving their performance on both the production and the marketing fronts. Although they may be part of an interdependent, oligopolistic market structure, they may have only a limited degree of market power. The strong competition may ensure that each firm seeks to satisfy the customer rather than to protect its own position. If this is the case, individual firms may be highly successful in terms of having a dynamic technological approach and a substantial market share, while having relatively little power to exploit the consumer.

However, if one business succeeds at the expense of its competitors, the situation may be very different. A price leader which can effectively drive competitors out of business, or merge with them, may acquire immense market power in the process. Depending upon how contestable the market is, that business may exploit this power by charging a higher price and restricting the quantity produced and sold.

Enquiry 2 looks in more detail at the ways in which businesses strive for success and the effect that this has upon their position in the market. Business success can be measured by profitability but this is not the whole story. Depending upon their objectives, success may be seen as maximising market share, or total sales. Often, the benefits of success in the market constitute a wider advantage. The rewards and rights of employees may increase. Contributions to the community are more likely. Concern for the environment may grow. Much depends on the firm's corporate culture. Enquiries 3 and 4 address these aspects of business behaviour while examining the market power of consumers, shareholders, managers and employees.

The UK government and the EU have policies which are designed to control and limit market power. These are the subject of Enquiry 5.

Open Question

What are the implications of the market power of business for the consumer?

Enquiry 2: How do businesses become powerful?

Scope

The ingredients of business success are very varied. However, there are a number of key factors which firms may be able to control. Efficient production strategies, high quality, carefully developed relationships with suppliers and dynamic marketing strategies can all contribute to success. Each of these key factors has many elements. There is also the possibility of merger, diversification or of concentration on what the company does best. It is possible to be successful in business without acquiring market power but, for many firms, it is market power which brings success.

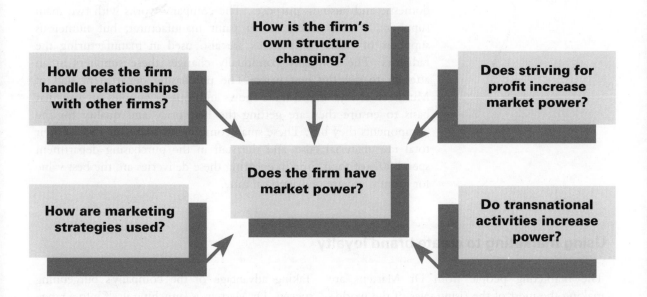

Opening evidence

Making a better mousetrap

'If a man write a better book, preach a better sermon, or make a better mousetrap than his neighbour, though he build his house in the woods, the world will make a beaten path to his door.'
— Ralph Emerson

Multitech Ltd

Multitech is a small manufacturing company located outside Newport in Gwent. It manufactures and assembles hot water radiators for domestic and business purposes. The company works with two main suppliers, a steel maker and a paint manufacturer, but numerous suppliers of small components are also used in manufacturing the radiators. The company continually changes these suppliers in an attempt to get the best price. The purchasing department staff of Multitech always attend trade shows and look at samples on a regular basis to ensure they are getting the best price and quality for the components they buy. These small components make up 15% of their total raw material costs and the staff in the purchasing department spend 90% of their time in ensuring these deliveries are the best value for money and are delivered on time.

Using marketing to create brand loyalty

The marketing people from Dr Martens are making the most of the rising sales of the world's twenty-sixth best-known brand.

Turnover in America has risen rapidly in the past three years, from £7m in 1990 to £38m in 1993 (total world sales in 1993 will be over £190m). The original products, the eight-eyelet boot and the three-eyelet shoe, account for 70% of the total output. This allows large economies of scale and easy identification with the brand image.

Taking advantage of the company's burgeoning success, Dr Martens is launching itself into a range of men's clothing. To be successful, the new label, DM Clothing, will need to have 'the lasting style, affordability and durability' which have made the footwear so successful. The market, identified as the type of clothes that men hang on to and are reluctant to throw away, is far from the fashion conscious styles of many designers. The range aims to take advantage of the Dr Martens image, but its début will be at Selfridges and Harrods, rather than the local street market.

UK mergers

The recent history of UK mergers shows a very noticeable cycle, both in terms of the number and the value of mergers.

	1985	1986	1987	1988	1989	1990	1991
Number of mergers	474	841	1,528	1,495	1,331	779	500
Expenditure (£m)	7,090	15,362	16,485	22,741	27,054	8,004	10,574

Source: Central Statistical Office

An FT leader

A YEAR after the startling decision by Philip Morris to cut the US price of Marlboro cigarettes, this response to collapsing sales looks much more than an isolated incident. Makers of most other branded consumer goods are finding that consumers are increasingly reluctant to pay premium prices for their products.

The surge in consumer spending which inflated branded manufacturers' profits and spurred a takeover frenzy in the late 1980s blinded them to fundamental shifts in the industry. What today seems a golden age was actually the swan song of outdated business methods.

Many companies are still struggling to escape from an industrial time warp. As some admit, their priorities have been dictated too much by the need to keep costly mass production lines busy and not enough by market demand. Their much-vaunted marketing departments have often become inward-looking bureaucracies, cut off from the real world. Innovation and consumer responsiveness have suffered as a result.

Many western industries, such as US car manufacturers, have grappled with similar problems since the early 1980s. Consumer goods producers have avoided them until recently for two reasons. One is the increasingly oligopolistic structure of their markets, in many of which no more than three suppliers can survive profitably.

The other is the lack of effective competition from Japanese and other Asian manufacturers, few of which have so far ventured into international markets.

But recession and the steadily growing power of supermarket chains have changed all that. This is especially true in the UK, where centralised buying and distribution have enabled supermarkets to drive increasingly hard bargains. Furthermore, their electronic sales information systems provide detailed marketing data long before it is available to manufacturers. As a consequence, a traditional contest between customers and suppliers has become a battle between different brands.

Source: *Financial Times*, 19 April 1994

Producer agreements can be difficult …

Aluminium smelters have been having problems. There has been over-capacity in the industry. The main cause of this has been the diversion of Russian production away from the domestic market and into exports. Prices on world markets fell and many were making losses.

In January 1994 a capacity-reducing agreement was made, involving representatives from governments and the industry. The Russian and western governments agreed to shut down 10% of capacity and prices rose by 30%. The companies lost as sales volumes fell but gained more from the price increases. They were happy: their position was improving and because governments were involved in the initial agreement they could not be accused of creating a cartel.

Aluminium cans await recycling.

Unfortunately, the improvement was partly illusory. Plant was mothballed in Europe, North America and Australia. But the Russian representatives who negotiated the deal did not have very much control over the Russian producers. No one knows whether they have kept to the agreement. The irony is that if prices had remained low, some Russian producers might have been driven out of the market anyway. Now with higher prices, they may survive. Western producers may feel like bringing some capacity back into production.

1 Relationships with suppliers

Within any company's chain of production the suppliers of components or raw materials are as important as the consumer of the product. If a company does not develop appropriate relationships with suppliers as well as customers, then things will not go well. Despite the suppliers treating the business as a customer, establishing some control over areas of component and raw material supply, such as delivery schedules, quality control, price levels, and so on, can have major benefits. In the long run, costs may be reduced.

Working with suppliers

An example of partnership sourcing

Glaxo is one UK company for which development of strategic alliances and partnerships has become a top priority. Glaxo's most sophisticated partnership, to date, is a five-year partnership with Courtaulds Packaging Betts and Company to supply a complex dispenser for a new medicine.

There were some reservations but openness and involvement by the consortium members, together with the clear mutual business benefits to be gained, led to close working relationships within the team. Once established, the development of multi-disciplinary links forged at design, manufacturing and even board level, maximised the benefits of the partnership. Furthermore, a willingness to manage not only success, but also failure, constructively when something went wrong at a supplier level was central to the partnership.

The result is that Glaxo benefits through the on-time development of highest quality components. Courtaulds Packaging Betts and Company gains through machine utilisation guarantees and all parties win by a commitment to improve productivity continuously and to share the benefits of reducing production costs.

Source: Adapted from CBI, *Report of the Manufacturing Advisory Group*, 1991

Traditionally, companies have encouraged adversarial relationships with their suppliers. Managers have often insisted upon three quotes, in writing, before anything can be ordered. Even when the company needs to re-order, the supplier who won the initial order will need to re-tender in case someone else is cheaper. This competitive system is rapidly being replaced by new relationships based upon trust. This philosophy is built upon the following premises:

- Supply will be long-term. This will enable the suppliers to plan for the future and improve their own production techniques via capital investment.
- Supply is mutually beneficial. Both the supplier and the manufacturer benefit from having well-established contracts. The supplier reduces the uncertainty of being in business and the manufacturer can make savings in the costs of production.
- Fewer suppliers are needed. It is much easier to work with a few other businesses, thereby creating better working relationships and there are fewer things that can go wrong.
- Better quality suppliers are needed. Businesses will only survive with good quality products and control over quality begins with the raw materials/components.
- Research and development and technical development can be pursued jointly with greater effect.

Just-in-time

Much thought lies behind this changing relationship and companies now recognise that their suppliers are very important in ensuring the quality of their own products. Indeed, if just-in-time stock control is to be introduced successfully, good relationships with suppliers are essential. However, to build up the necessary trust and commitment to these mutually beneficial contracts takes a long time.

Once the company is happy with its suppliers, there are many potential savings and reductions in waste. Some of these savings can easily be seen. Increased scope for the use of just-in-time strategies means that the company will have less need for storeroom space and, hence, there is less need to move goods from holding areas to storerooms to the shopfloor.

Suppliers are often small companies. A large customer company can have substantial market power. It will be able to bargain on price and quantity specifications. It will probably force the smaller company, which may have few alternative customers, to accept prices which drive profits down to the minimum needed to stay in business. On the other hand, the long term relationship with the customer company will give some degree of security which would previously have been lacking.

Subcontracting

An increasingly popular way of organising large businesses is to subcontract work a company has previously done itself. This has always happened within the building industry and in some service industries but it is now part of every large company's range of options. Often, the subcontractor can achieve cost savings that were impossible for the company itself.

Guardia Ltd

Guardia is a medium-sized firm of builders, based in Clwyd. The private, family-run company employs 20 staff but uses over 150 subcontractors from within the building industry. Most of these subcontractors are self-employed tradespeople or small partnerships. The full-time staff of 20 are responsible for co-ordinating all the building contracts, which amount to over £1.2 million per year. In 1990 the directors of the company became concerned about the amount of administration being undertaken by the 20 permanent members of staff and tried to find ways of solving the problem. Their solution was to reduce the number of staff to 18 and buy in freelance help. The present situation involves the 18 employees working in their specialist roles, tendering for new business and checking up on the quality of work done. The freelancers take care of payment of salaries, collection of moneys owed, cleaning, legal work, the preparation of contracts for subcontractors and computer services.

In proposing this solution to the problem of excess paperwork, the directors hoped to save money as well as to allow their staff to concentrate on the areas where they were most productive and efficient.

Businesses have used subcontracting to reduce the personnel involved in central services such as the accounts department, office cleaning or delivery. There may be huge advantages in employing a specialist service agency to cover work previously done in-house. It is one more example of specialisation and the division of labour.

This process is visible in the big increase in self-employment which occurred during the 1980s. People who previously worked for large employers have shifted to freelancing, often for the same employer. Some are working for lower incomes, reflecting the large company's power in the market for business services. Others have found that improved productivity enables them to earn more.

2 How businesses collaborate in the market

There are many ways in which businesses can work together, both legitimately and anti-competitively. Some of these methods can be represented by the series of steps shown in Figure 2.1.

Figure 2.1 Ways in which firms collaborate

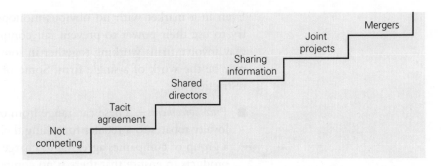

Open Question

Why might collaboration between firms be against the public interest?

Within this hierarchy of collaboration, some techniques are explicit and other competitors will be aware of what is happening. Other practices arise on an informal level, usually because they contravene UK and EU legislation on collusion and anti-competitive behaviour. **Collusion** implies that the collaboration is against the public interest and it is therefore likely to be concealed.

One form of collusion involves a restrictive practice known as a **tacit agreement**. This involves no negotiation or formal agreement. There will be no written evidence or contractual obligation for the businesses to continue their collaboration. The organisations concerned will be aware that they cannot rely on the agreement. They will simply continue to behave in ways which avoid causing trouble for each other. Frequently, a tacit agreement takes the form of both companies avoiding price cuts and opting for non–price competition of various kinds. If the agreement comes to an end, the result may be a price war. This kind of scenario is very typical of oligopolies.

Restrictive practices

When one or more companies try to take advantage of their market power to prevent competition, they are said to be operating a **restrictive practice**.

Ready-mixed concrete

Early in 1994, a group of ready-mixed concrete producers was accused of making price-fixing and market-sharing agreements in different parts of England. The managers of competing firms had agreed not to compete on price and had also avoided competing in particular geographical areas. Some of them had been found guilty of these practices three years previously and had been fined a total of £56,000. One of the companies said it had issued instructions to staff not to participate in any market-sharing arrangement as any such activity is against the law.

Even in a market with no obvious monopoly elements, businesses can try to use their power to prevent fair competition. Restrictive practices may involve firms working together in some form of collusion, or they may be the work of a single firm. Some of the more common types of restriction are:

- *Price agreements* – These can range from one company providing loyalty rebates to a retailer for selling their products to customers, to a group of companies agreeing to charge a common price for their products to ensure that there is no competition.
- *Output fixing agreements* – These are often part of a **cartel** arrangement where a group of businesses restrict their own output to make the products relatively scarce. The price is then forced higher, which benefits each company. OPEC is an example of a legal cartel that attempted to control the price of oil by restricting output.
- *Regional agreements* – Firms may agree not to compete in each other's home market, thereby allowing each business to have the benefits of a regional monopoly. Company A might supply Scotland, company B the North of England, etc. However, just because a company is strong in one area of the country does not mean there is any agreement between competitors.
- *Control of retail outlets* – Some powerful businesses will try to prevent competition by restricting access to retail outlets. This can be seen with the control over beer supplied in many pubs in the UK.
- Firms can hinder competition by using lobbyists, specialist knowledge and contacts, etc. Some of these are perfectly legitimate; others are not.

Open Question

How might restrictive practices affect consumers?

OPEC

An example of an effective cartel has been the Organisation of Petroleum Exporting Countries (OPEC). It was set up to control the output of the oil producing nations in the Middle East. During the 1970s, this cartel was very successful in controlling the world's output of oil and, consequently, it was able to increase prices to a large extent. This was one of the causes of the high rate of inflation experienced in the UK in 1975 as oil prices had risen by 400% in 1973–74. The success and effectiveness of OPEC as a cartel has declined since then because of the discovery of new sources of oil outside the Middle East. The Gulf War of 1991 saw the end of the cartel as a force in the market, at least for the time being.

The role of the government in controlling and preventing restrictive practices is taken up in Enquiry 5.

Mergers and takeovers

No deal: Sweden's Volvo and France's Renault decided not to go ahead with their planned merger.

Renault–Volvo

The new company of Renault–Volvo planned to begin its operations in January 1994. The two car and lorry manufacturers expected to join together in an attempt to compete with their larger rivals. Despite producing 2.4 million vehicles per year (12.1% share of the world market), the company would still be only the fifth largest in the world.

The companies had worked together on a number of joint projects since 1990 and the merger plans followed an increasing trend in car production world-wide. The pressures facing these two businesses had arisen from both American and Japanese firms, plus the potential opening up of the European Union market to outside producers in the year 2000.

The merger never happened. The Volvo shareholders began to suspect that the deal was more favourable to the Renault shareholders than to them. Although the merger might well have made commercial sense, they refused to agree to it and the plans were abandoned. The Volvo managers who had set up the deal were replaced.

Reasons for mergers

Horizontal, vertical, lateral and conglomerate mergers

Mergers occur for many different reasons, and sometimes for reasons which turn out to be rather weakly founded. Firms in related lines of business often merge. When they do, particularly if it is a horizontal merger, there is a real possibility of the merged business gaining enhanced market power.

In many markets the potential economies of scale have been so huge that merger was essential if prices were to be brought down. In some industries the minimum efficient scale is such that there will be room for only a small number of mass producers. Then mergers have an important role to play in the rationalisation of the industry. Inevitably, however, once there are just a few players in the market, each will have significant market power.

Synergy

Focus

Many takeover bids and subsequent mergers occur when the stock exchange is rising (i.e. when there is a bull market) and business confidence is buoyant. Some of these mergers can turn out to have been mistaken. The promised benefits are not realised and, in some cases, the merged companies have split up again. Some companies have found themselves to be so diversified by acquisitions that they lose focus. The pharmaceuticals company Zeneca was part of ICI until 1993, but was split off in this way. Thorn EMI has been actively involved in both mergers and divestments (when parts of the business are sold off).

Thorn EMI

Between 1985 and 1993, Thorn EMI sold 80 of its subsidiaries in order to concentrate on what it does best: recording and publishing music, and renting out items ranging from TVs to jewellery.

The music side of the business has on its books the Pet Shop Boys, Paula Abdul and Genesis, among others. It has 22% of the worldwide music market. The most profitable part of the business is Virgin Music, bought from Richard Branson in early 1992. By combining Virgin's manufacturing and distribution activities with those of EMI Music, the group benefited from the synergy created.

Thorn EMI has been keen to expand its music business further. Late in 1993 it acquired the rights to manage ATV Music, a music publishers owned by Michael Jackson.

The only cloud on the horizon is in the shape of investigations into the price of CDs in the USA, by the Federal Trade Commission.

The many possible reasons for merging include:

1 *Economies of scale* – One advantage of larger organisations is the ability to produce larger outputs and hence make savings on the costs of production.

2 *Spreading of risk* – By moving into new areas of business, i.e. diversifying, the companies can avoid 'putting all their eggs in one basket.' These are conglomerate mergers, e.g. R.J. Reynolds and Nabisco, enabling the companies to operate in the food and tobacco markets.

3 *Synergy* – Businesses often believe that the sum of the parts is less than the whole and that by bringing different businesses together there will be value added that is greater than the former parts. This was a particularly strong motive in the 1980s and a well known example is Habitat joining with Mothercare and British Home Stores. Unfortunately, potential synergy is often overestimated.

4 *Rationalisation* – Examples of mergers that occurred for this reason can be seen in the building societies. They have been able to rationalise the number of branches to make savings.

5 *Marketing strategy* – In some ways a merger is like developing a new product that can add vitality to an existing range of goods. Sometimes businesses will seek to merge, rather than developing new products, as

a short cut to entering a market where they have ambitions. If they wish to enter the US market with a well known product it might be quicker and easier to merge with a US-based business.

6 *Asset stripping* – A company whose asset values, as shown by the balance sheet, are less than their value when the company is split up and sold, is ripe for takeovers or mergers. Hanson plc has been cited as a follower of this practice.

7 *Rewards for managers* – When mergers take place, new, more senior, jobs are created and these can be attractive to managers seeking to improve their own position. If the merger is successful, it is a quick way of raising the management's profile and fame.

8 *Defensive motives* – Businesses which are feeling vulnerable to takeover may seek another company with whom to merge. This makes the other takeover less likely and their position more secure; they choose their partners themselves.

Open Question

Have recent mergers increased the market power of the firms concerned?

Takeover or develop new products?

Companies differ in their views as to whether it is better to develop their own product range or to take over an existing business and buy into the product range that way. Japanese companies nearly always develop their own new products and takeovers play a very small part in corporate strategy. In the UK, takeovers are more frequent and a part of 'normal' business activity. Some of the advantages of a takeover are related to the high status and the increasing profile associated with it, as well as the ability to take a short cut.

Research has shown that roughly 50% of takeovers fail to achieve the gains that were hoped for. If the people who brought about the takeover did so for reasons of personal prestige, it is hardly surprising if the outcome is disappointing.

However, even if there were powerful commercial motives for merging, the merged company may still perform relatively poorly. Synergy may fail to materialise. A loss of focus may mean that the business is attempting to enter markets in which it does not have a competitive advantage. The merger may have been a one-off activity and not part of the company's overall strategy. Sometimes too much emphasis is given to past financial performance and not enough to consideration of the future potential.

Thorn EMI provides an interesting example of some of these factors. Having expanded considerably and diversified, it returned to a policy of seeking focus. At the same time, it took over other businesses within its field of expertise.

Joint projects

Two or more businesses can come together for a specific advertising programme or other activity. Sometimes they can create a new third company in which they both own the shares. These joint projects can be short-term, such as Persil and Hotpoint sharing the costs of television adverts, or they can be permanent, such as two oil companies sharing the risk of exploring for new oil reserves in Alaska. Some joint projects can involve the setting up of new businesses: Boots and WH Smith came together to form the Do-It-All chain of paint and decorating retail outlets.

Video rivals seek format accord

JAPAN'S biggest electronics rivals, Sony and Matsushita, are holding talks about the coming generation of high definition digital video tape recorders to avoid the bruising marketing battle previously suffered when consumers were presented with two incompatible systems. All the main Japanese appliance companies are talking and Phillips of the Netherlands and Thomson of France are likely to join in, according to reports from Japan. Matsushita said in a statement: 'We are currently in discussions with Sony and other companies about our mutual desire to form a single, world-wide format.'

Almost 20 years ago, Sony introduced its Betamax format for video cassette recorders, winning applause for technical quality. Other companies at first accepted Sony's format. But Matsushita, coming to the battle late, adopted the VHS format, developed by its own subsidiary. It was joined by other companies, and their greater marketing muscle in Japan meant that VHS became the standard system. Research costs for the new generation of VCRs are so high that no company wants to go it alone and get it wrong.

Source: Adapted from the *Guardian*, 16 February 1993

Vertical integration

Vertical integration has been an important motive for mergers in the past. Companies saw it as a way of guaranteeing supplies and sometimes also markets. The changes in supplier relationships, detailed earlier in this Enquiry, mean that this sort of merger has become less frequent.

The holiday market

The package holiday industry is organised in two sections: the retail outlets which sell the holidays and the companies which provide the holidays. The four big tour operators, Airtours, Thomson Holidays, Owners Abroad and Thomas Cook, dominate the market. Each of these operators tries to sell as many holidays as possible and they promote their products heavily with the travel agents as well as the public. The travel agents, again dominated by a few large chains of retail outlets, are not always independent businesses. At the time of writing, Pickfords Travel and Hogg Robinson (since renamed Going Places Leisure Travel) had 550 high street shops and were owned by Airtours. Lunn Poly, owned by Thomson Holidays, sells one in three of all UK package holidays. Thomas Cook, with its chain of 340 retail outlets, owned 20% of Owners Abroad.

3 Striving for profits and growth

Whatever their long-term aims, most businesses want to be efficient and to achieve a competitive advantage. Cutting costs through JIT and improved management strategies can increase profits. It can also lead to reduced prices which can help to capture an increased market share. Having cut prices, the business can justifiably claim to have the consumers' interests at heart, yet the end result of this is that the business also has enhanced market power. The larger its market share, the more likely it is to be able to influence the market and reduce the power of competitors.

An alternative approach to achieving improved competitive advantage is to increase the benefits to the consumer so that they get better value for money. Efforts to improve quality contribute to this.

Organic growth

The quest for new markets leads firms into new ventures in other countries. They set up distribution systems for their exports. In time they may decide to produce in the country to which they have been exporting. Alternatively, they may buy locally based companies. In these ways they become transnational corporations (TNCs), firms with activities in more than one country. Often, the sheer size of the resulting company gives it some market power.

This section looks, in turn, at production, quality control and the effect of transnationals.

Just-in-time

The just-in-time (JIT) philosophy transfers many of the storage problems associated with manufacturing to the component suppliers. By insisting on regular and frequent deliveries, the manufacturer buys only enough parts for the immediate needs of the business. Components arrive in time to be used and this eliminates the need for storage facilities and a large warehousing department. This process of supplying components only when they are needed also extends along the production line. The resulting close relationship with suppliers may or may not lead to the large customer company exploiting its market power.

Team work and continuous improvement

Team working has been an important development in manufacturing in the 1980s and 1990s. Volvo, early pioneers of such an approach, found that the resulting increased efficiency enabled them to compete in the international car market despite their relatively small size. Team working is part of a package of measures within which continuous improvement is the prime focus.

Kaizen

The introduction of Japanese-style working relations in British-based businesses has transformed many of the UK's traditional working patterns. These changes have particularly affected assembly work on conveyor belts.

A typical change has involved employees working in teams of eight under the supervision of a team leader. Each team is given the responsibility and authority to design their own jobs. Working collectively, each team will discover ways to improve the production flow, increase the quality of the product and improve their own working conditions. This belief in teams which are multi-skilled attempts to motivate staff and recognises the value of employees. The process of continual improvement alongside standardised work – **kaizen** – is part of the modern manufacturing system.

Each team is encouraged to reduce waste wherever possible while following the standardised procedures established by the team leader, in consultation with the team. Each team finds improved ways of doing things and the approach is continually refined and developed. Ultimately, kaizen is about job ownership and giving employees full responsibility and authority for their own jobs. They have the responsibility for producing high standard products and, in return, they receive the authority necessary to change their ways of working so as to ensure high standards and high productivity.

Employee involvement

Many companies have seen the advantage of 'empowering' employees to take more responsibility for their work, both in terms of controlling costs and ensuring quality. Some managers have recognised that their staff, have considerable expertise and a more comprehensive knowledge of the day-to-day activity within the factory. To get the best from the staff, these skills need to be respected and encouraged. (This is looked at in more detail in Enquiry 4.)

Ensuring quality

BS5750 is a British Standard that gives guidelines on quality systems. It involves the careful documentation of the correct way to do everything within the organisation. This includes how to answer the phone, how to respond to a customer inquiry, how to prepare the company accounts, etc. The registered inspectors then check that the company follows its own procedures and, if so, BS5750 is awarded. This is very much a system, in that the standard is merely for following your own company's policy. It does not mean that the policy is necessarily of a high standard, just that the employees can, and do, follow it.

Figure 2.2 Symbol of quality: the BSI kitemark

Source: British Standards Institute

Open Question

What effect will quality improvements have on the consumer?

The British Standards Institute (BSI) also provides industry with product certification as well as quality assurance concerning the company's procedures. The BSI kitemark, as shown in Figure 2.2, is well recognised as a sign of quality – it indicates that BSI has tested the product and confirmed compliance with the appropriate standard. BSI hopes that the standard BS5750 will become equally recognised.

Total quality management

This is a systematic approach to looking at all of a company's activities in an attempt to seek improvement. It is a way of improving the effectiveness, flexibility and competitiveness of the business as a whole. It involves each department and each individual in improving processes and procedures. Because each person affects, and is affected by, others, it is necessary for the whole organisation to collaborate. The approach needs the commitment of the whole organisation, a culture of 'get-it-right-first-time' and good internal communications.

All businesses have to pay attention to the quality of their processes and products. In some companies this is handled systematically through a total quality management (TQM) approach, which has been fashionable for several years and is recommended by many management consultants. However, it is by no means the only possible approach to quality control.

All of these measures to improve company performance have a role to play in strengthening the ability of the business to withstand competition. They are dealt with very briefly here because they are covered in detail elsewhere, but their contribution towards the growth of market power should be kept in mind.

Transnational expansion

International business has existed for thousands of years, however both the growth and the changing nature of international trade have been highly significant since the end of the Second World War. It is now estimated that transnational companies (TNCs) account for 70–80% of the world's trade. Sometimes the motive for setting up in another country is to produce for a significant market in that country. Often, the motive has to do with production costs. In particular, much foreign investment is aimed at reducing labour costs by moving production to a country with lower wage rates. Some countries, such as South Korea, developed so fast as a result of foreign investment that standards of living rose fast and wage rates rose too. They have gradually ceased to be low-wage economies.

The multiplier

There are a number of advantages for a country in playing host to investment by overseas companies. These apply just as much for Japanese businesses setting up in the UK as they do for a multinational based in the EU setting up in Africa. When international investment brings additional spending to a particular locality, a multiplier effect occurs. The initial injection is respent in another sector of the economy. There is a local upward multiplier effect.

There are also some disadvantages for the host country. There may be some loss of sovereignty: because multinational companies (MNCs) are often very powerful the ability of a government to control the destiny of the country can be affected. This applies mainly to small, developing countries or those with unstable governments.

International trade and foreign investment by TNCs can both create and reduce market power. A company with subsidiaries in many countries can have immense market power simply because of its financial resources. In general, however, more international trade means more competition and this usually reduces market power. Each situation has to be weighed up individually.

Where TNCs develop a degree of market power, it usually has a number of specific aspects. Enhanced economies of scale, particularly in marketing, can create an advantage. (The degree of world-wide brand recognition for products such as Coca-Cola is an example.) The capacity to locate labour-intensive stages in the production sequence in countries with low labour costs gives another advantage. Bargaining power with both suppliers and distributors is a significant factor.

4 Marketing strategies

In seeking to obtain a competitive advantage, marketing strategies are highly important. Through them, the firm tries to make its market more imperfect. It differentiates the product. It may, through advertising, accentuate this differentiation in the consumer's perception. The marketing mix is really all about beating the competition, the impact of which it aims to reduce.

Marketing can be used to increase market share or at least to increase product recognition. The first stage is to identify appropriate objectives and the different strategies available. There are no right answers because the best way will depend on such factors as the type of industry, the level of competition, the company's image and the economic climate. Deciding on an appropriate strategy could involve

SWOT analysis (strengths, weaknesses, opportunities and threats) or an examination of the **key factors** for success. These approaches enable the management to identify how well the business can compete in existing and future markets.

As a consequence of using SWOT or key factor analysis, businesses are able to identify enough information about their own organisation, and the competitor's, to design a plan of action. Any strategy should answer the fundamental question of 'why should customers buy our products or services rather than the competitor's?'

There are a large number of different ways of meeting the company's strategic aims. Charging a high price and competing on quality, together with a strong advertising effort aimed at giving widespread brand recognition, is a combination of strategies used by many well-known companies. Perfume manufacturers have achieved a good deal of control over their markets in this way.

Alternatively, penetration pricing can increase market share, and hence market power, with high volumes and lower margins acting as a barrier to entry. Surf washing powder has been marketed in this way. Innovative product development, exploitation of niche markets, imaginative advertising campaigns and myriad less-obvious strategies can be employed to place the company beyond the threat of competing products.

Each of these approaches can be categorised using the type of competitive advantage identified by Michael Porter and summarised in Enquiry 1 on p. 24.

The strategic marketing mix

The marketing mix identifies the essential techniques involved in selling a product or service. The ingredients of the marketing mix (often called the four Ps), price, product, promotion and place (distribution), can be used to influence or control the market. By looking at the elements of the marketing mix, it is possible to see how a business continually adjusts to changes in market circumstances with a view to achieving its strategic aims.

Price

An application of pricing strategies to the enhancement of market power can be seen when **predatory pricing** is employed. Supposing there are new entrants to the market. They may undercut the prices of existing suppliers. A possible response is to make even deeper price cuts.

Variable costs may still be covered but if a price war develops then an absolute loss, with price below variable costs, may deliberately be accepted. The goal of the larger established firms is to bleed their competitors to death financially. When the new entrant finally leaves the market, the original firms will restore prices close to previous levels.

Predatory pricing may, then, succeed in driving the new entrants out again. This is what happened to Laker Airways. Alternatively, over time one business may develop to the point where it can contemplate driving out competitors of long standing.

Laker Airways

Until the early 1970s, the airlines effectively operated a cartel. They charged high prices which many people could not afford. Their planes were often half empty but, nevertheless, the price charged kept them quite profitable.

Along came Freddie Laker. An ex-airline pilot, his ambition was to own a successful airline. Normally, airlines would be described as having very major barriers to entry. But Laker succeeded. He offered cut-price travel to North America, filling his planes to capacity. At last people on relatively ordinary incomes could travel at prices they could afford. The airline grew rapidly.

The large, established airlines were aghast. They had no inclination to compete but they were losing business. They had no option. They reduced their own prices even further. They accepted a period of loss making in order to take over business from Laker Airways.

Eventually, they succeeded in undercutting Laker for long enough to force the company into liquidation. However, just a few years later there was another new entrant …

By contrast, the firm which seeks to establish and hold a commanding market position may try to keep its price low enough to ensure having a substantial market share. If it is operating in a market which is to any extent contestable, any tendency to earn super normal profit will bring new entrants into the market. **Deterrent pricing** avoids this: the price is kept too low for the market to be attractive. Thus a market may be contestable but still have only a few competitors, all behaving in ways which respect the fact that there would be new entrants if the price were higher.

Product

Developing the product offers considerable scope for increasing market power. Product positioning is an attempt to find a segment of the market which is poorly catered for. Self-evidently, its being so means that there will be less competition within that market segment. However, doing this successfully requires being sure to keep in close touch with the market so that consumers' needs really are met effectively.

Market segmentation

By definition, the niche market is one that the main competitors in the field have chosen to ignore. It therefore creates a small, but less competitive market. Within it, the producer may have some market power.

As products and consumer expectations evolve, many businesses feel that, far from exploiting their market power, they are having to come up with new ideas just in order to survive. There is sometimes a fine line between achieving a position of some control over the market and simply staying in business. Survival may require a constant watch being kept over the new product lines of competitors.

Product development may mean actually searching for new products, as happens in the pharmaceutical industry where there is constant research for new and more effective drugs. Or it may mean improving an existing product to make it more attractive or more reliable, effectively prolonging the product life-cycle in the way shown in Figure 2.3. The curve can be shifted from A to A_1 by relaunching the product in a new design, by more advertising or by increasing product appeal in another way.

Figure 2.3 Product life-cycle

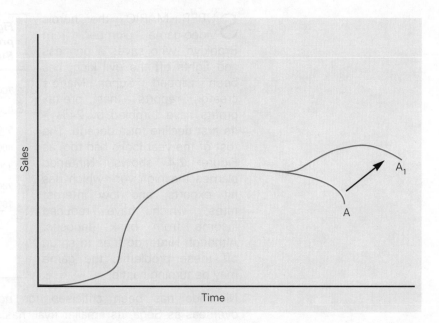

New product development

A genuinely new product may, for a time, create a degree of monopoly for its producer. Later, 'me-too' products will emerge to compete with it, but the firm that can keep up a continuous flow of new and different products will have a substantial competitive advantage. Rivals may find it difficult to keep up, particularly if there are legal restraints, such as copyrights or patents, associated with the new developments.

All research and development involves risks, so the successful company will seek ways of minimising them. One way of doing this is to aim for continuous product modifications, especially if the life–cycle of the product is short. Another aspect of new product development involves carefully relating the new product to consumer demand. This may be achieved by skilful analysis of the market. Alternatively it may involve advertising and promoting the product in such a way that consumer demand is created.

In electronic games manufacturing, all these features are significant in determining the market power of the contestants. The successful company has to have a complex strategy which takes care of all aspects of marketing. However, the prizes for a firm which succeeds in dominating the market are enormous.

Open Question

To what extent does new product development benefit the consumer?

Nintendo

SUPER MARIO, the heroic video-game plumber from Brooklyn, who saves a princess and fights off the evil king, has been zapped. Super Mario's creator reports that pre-tax profits have tumbled by 24% – its first decline for a decade. The rest of the year looks bad too, as Figure 2.4 shows. Nintendo blames the high yen, which has hit exports, and low interest rates, which have reduced income from bank deposits. Although Nintendo tries to shrug off these problems, the game may be turning nastier.

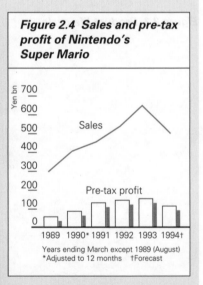

Figure 2.4 Sales and pre-tax profit of Nintendo's Super Mario

Years ending March except 1989 (August)
*Adjusted to 12 months †Forecast

Nintendo has been criticised for not transferring production overseas as Sega, its smaller rival, has done. Sega now produces half its games machines elsewhere, mostly in South-East Asia, which is why it expects profits to increase in the year to March 1994 to ¥57.5 billion on sales of ¥380 billion (although this is still a lower profit margin than market-leading Nintendo).

Hiroshi Yamauchi, Nintendo's president, says his firm intends to open a factory in China, but mainly to supply the local market. He believes having factories overseas is not a good idea because it is hard to ensure rigorous quality control. So far, his ideas have been good for Nintendo, allowing what was a maker of playing cards to capture 70% of the world's $8 billion market for home video games. But Nintendo may now need a new game plan.

As part of its strategy, Nintendo sells its hardware at close to cost price, making most of its money from expensive software. Nintendo's customers (mostly six- to 18-year-olds) are far more interested in the fun they get out of games than the machines needed to run them, says Mr Yamauchi. In America, the company typically sells a game machine for about $100 and a cartridge containing the game's software for about $70. This tactic no longer seems to be working. Demand for a new, more powerful 16-bit games machine has levelled off much earlier than expected. This could be because the games seem dull. Nintendo licensed lots of software firms, who were keen to rush into the games business, to produce them. Many found they could not afford the increasing time and cost of originality. Ten years ago it took a pair of computer programmers six months to complete a new game; nowadays it can take a team of 20 two years.

The market has also been flooded with 'me-too' versions of Nintendo games. In October Japan's Capcom filed a lawsuit against Data East for infringing the copyright on its 'Street Fighter II' software. Prices have also fallen. Video-game freaks in Tokyo's Akihabara district have been buying games at discounts of up to 80%.

Meanwhile, Sega has launched a new marketing offensive. A TV ad it has been running in America features slow-witted people playing a Nintendo hand-held Game Boy while a voice-over intones: 'Some people are content to be entertained by simple one-colour electronics. Somehow these people have just never heard of Game Gear'. This is the name of Sega's more sophisticated, and pricier, hardware. Its software is also harder-hitting: the firm's version of 'Mortal Kombat' has hearts being ripped out of bodies and victim's heads being chopped off. Nintendo objects to extreme violence in games.

How long Nintendo can defend such principles remains to be seen. Its rivals are already launching new generations of 32-bit games machines and developing 64-bit versions to follow. These could blow Mario's mind. They have movie-like images in three dimensions and slick controls, including some that are voice activated. America's 3DO already has an advanced games machine on the market, though at a whopping $699. Atari will launch its Jaguar later this year; Sony has set up a new joint venture to market a 32-bit machine. Sega has teamed up with Hitachi to develop new machines.

Source: Adapted from *The Economist*, 20 November 1993

Open Question

Who has power in the video games market?

The end result of new product development in some markets is product proliferation. There may be no niches left. From time to time, one firm may emerge from the crowd and take a dominating position for a while. Quite quickly, though, its competitors will catch up with new products of their own, eroding the position of the market leader. This state of affairs can bring major benefits to the consumer if the competing firms are making genuine efforts to meet demand in meaningful ways. However, many consumer durables now come in so many designs and variants that it is difficult for the consumer to decide which is likely to offer the best buy.

Legal protections available

Many businesses can take advantage of unique elements within their product design or the process of production. The law recognises that businesses that invest in design and research have the right to be protected from competitors. A number of laws give businesses this protection. The Copyright, Design and Patents Act of 1988 provides for people who create new products or processes to be entitled to:

1 own them
2 control their use and protect them against unauthorised use
3 receive acknowledgement for them
4 receive economic reward for their use.

There are minor differences between the two main areas of the Act in that when a company makes an advance in technology, it has to apply to the Patents Office to have a patent granted. If the patent is granted, the company is given the exclusive rights to this idea for 20 years. Copyright, however, comes into existence automatically when someone writes or designs new work. Copyright applies to written works, speeches, artistic works and designs.

Promotion: brands

Brand names have always been a way of creating customer loyalty as they enable the customer to identify products easily. In addition, the existence of the names creates certain expectations of satisfaction, or consumer surplus, in the minds of customers. Established brand names are a major intangible asset for some firms.

A branded product will be carefully positioned in the market in such a way as to develop associations in the customer's mind with quality, good value, reliability or any other important feature. Over time, brands evolve. Brand loyalty may wane. Without it, the brand name will have little market power but a relaunch can give a brand of long standing a new and dynamic image.

In recent years, brand loyalty has been on the wane generally, although it is still important in some markets. The response of one cigarette manufacturer is shown in the following case study.

Marlboro

In April 1993, Philip Morris, the owners of Marlboro, cut the price of their cigarettes in the USA. The effect of this was for all the tobacco companies selling in the USA to follow suit. This move to reduce the price of branded cigarettes in the USA has occurred because of the large price difference between 'cheap and cheerful' makes and the well-known brands. This difference ($2 compared to 80 cents) has accounted for the growth in market share of the non-branded cigarettes, up from 15% in 1988 to 41% in 1993.

To maintain a difference in price, large companies need to continue with their expensive advertising campaigns, without which they may not be able to justify their premium prices. For example, the owners of Camel cigarettes spent $23 million advertising their famous brand in 1992, all for a product that has just 3% of the US market. This trend to lower-priced, non-brand cigarettes has also occurred in the UK. In 1982 nearly 100% of the UK market was made up of 'full-price' brand-name cigarettes. In 1993 their share of the market was down to 58% because of the introduction of products such as Red Band, sold in cash and carry outlets.

During the second half of the 1980s, consumers were willing to pay high prices for the right label or image, a trend that has now changed markedly. The recession of the early 1990s made conspicuous consumption appear vulgar and, hence, the value of brand names to companies' asset values has fallen rapidly. While it may have been chic to wear designer labels on clothes in the 1980s, changing consumer values have made this habit less popular. The 1990s saw a marked reduction in the importance of brand names.

Promotion: advertising

Price elasticities, revenue and advertising

One way to improve market penetration is to advertise in imaginative ways. Advertising can both shift the demand curve to the right and make it more inelastic by improving the market perception of the product in comparison to substitutes. This, in turn, means that a price increase will be more likely to generate extra revenue. In itself, this increases market power.

In some industries, firms advertise as a matter of routine, purely in order to survive at all. Where advertising expenditure has become a significant proportion of total cost, it may become a barrier to entry. No potential new entrant will be big enough to have the marketing economies of scale needed to break in.

Recent trends have begun to take a different turn. The development of huge supermarket chains, which market themselves as retailers, has reduced the significance of brands and increased the share of own–brand labels. A supermarket chain which builds up an image of quality can make its own-brands credible as well as inexpensive.

The supermarkets have also developed substantial market power, partly through their corporate advertising. Sainsbury's experience with a TV campaign featuring recipes shows how advertising can be used to increase market share.

Sainsbury lures with a new lime

UNTIL this summer, limes were the things fashion-victims stuffed down the necks of beer bottles and tried to drink through, in a doomed attempt to look cool. But you may have noticed that, this year, limes are in. Want a tang in your salad dressing or a bit of spice in your marinade? Want to impress your dinner party guests? Then add lime.

Ever since Sainsbury brought recipe-in-a-commercial infomercials to the UK airwaves two years ago, the nation's leading grocer has been shifting vast quantities of its products.

When Selina Scott first purred out a recipe for pasta, six months' supply of mozzarella disappeared in one week. When Robert Morley rolled his eyes at Filo pastry just before Christmas, the entire country sold out. When John Nettles, a.k.a. Bergerac, threw pepperoni into some omelette, that week Sainsbury sold seven times its normal volume. Before Sainsbury talked about it crème fraiche hardly existed as a product: sales are up eightfold, albeit from a previously tiny base.

Likewise, when Sue Lawley introduced us to the delights of 'pepper crusted fish in a warm lime and coriander vinaigrette' in April, sales of limes doubled. According to Sainsbury research, in the weeks after the recipe advertisement was aired, each night 150,000 households sat down to eat Ms Lawley's dish.

While consumer groups worry about just how impressionable we all are, Sainsbury suppliers, who include the world's biggest and most sophisticated branded goods marketers, also have cause for concern – Sainsbury is beating them at their own game. Sainsbury has already got down to a fine art ideas that many marketers are still debating.

Idea number one: being consumer-led is *passé*. To be led by consumers is to be always one step behind. Instead, innovate, and lead them.

Idea number two: to deliver what your customers want is to be predictable and boring. Deliver what they do not know they want. Exceed expectations; delight them.

Peter Dart, a marketing consultant at the Added Value Company, says: 'Modern marketing is about manipulating the consumer into a new state, which is actually to their own interests. You are there not only to respond to customer needs but to lead their needs.'

David Abbott, the chairman and creative director of Abbott Mead Vickers and the bright spark who thought up the idea, says the Sainsbury advertisements were about 'the joy of cooking, which is why we chose the music and the pace. But we also wanted to stretch horizons without being too expensive or intricate'.

Idea number three: leave pure image advertising behind with the rest of the 1980s baggage. Use your product to enhance your brand values: quality, value for money, price and choice. Selina Scott may purr, Dennis Healey may raise his eyebrows, but in Sainsbury advertisements, while celebrities are important, 'the food is hero'.

Idea number four: do not just sell; build relationships. Recipes are a help to those doing the cooking: 'It is very simple, but we are effectively giving something back to the customer,' a Sainsbury spokesperson said. 'What all the ads have in common is what we call the three As: affordable, accessible and aspirational.'

Idea number five: distinctions between 'above-the-line' costs (advertising) and 'below-the-line' costs (the rest) are out of date. Clever marketers go through the line and integrate their marketing. At Sainsbury, the campaign is 'co-ordinated marketing at its best', including the four Ps: promotion (the recipe on national TV); place (strong point-of-sale material in stores); price (special offers on featured goods); and the product featured on recipe leaflets – 35 million of them so far.

Idea number six: leverage – why buy so much media space when you can use public relations to multiply the impact of smaller spending?

Source: Adapted from
The Times, 4 August 1993

Open Questions

Do 'infomercials' inform or persuade? What can advertising do for the market power of supermarket chains?

Place

There are a number of ways of using the distribution system to enhance market power, although some fall foul of legislation on restrictive practices. Distribution channels are themselves a significant barrier to entry. Small or local companies often find it very difficult to obtain a distribution contract. Indeed 'getting a listing' with the supermarkets is a critical threshold for a product's commercial success and effective entry to the product life-cycle.

Full-line forcing requires the retailer to stock and display the full product range of the manufacturer. Retailers then do not have the freedom to pick and choose which items they want to stock because the manufacturer will refuse to supply them on that basis. Independent retailers are too small to resist this kind of pressure.

Display creates other opportunities. Wrigley's chewing gum has been accused of putting competitors displays into less prominent positions in retail outlets. For this, the company was taken to task by the Office of Fair Trading but, by then, competitors had been pushed into the background for some time.

When Mars tried to break into the ice-cream market, they found that Walls were providing most small retailers with freezers in which to keep the product and refusing to let them keep any other company's products in them. The retailers had to get another freezer if they wanted to stock Mars products.

Conclusion

The link between business performance and market power cannot be denied. There is a tension between the interests of the successful business and the interests of the customer. However, many business managers consider that working in the interests of the customer is also good business practice. The next Enquiry looks at the ways in which consumers can control what happens in the market place and the extent to which control is possible.

This Enquiry concludes with a case study of a rather unusual firm. Its marketing mix is highly selective. It does not attempt to compete on price, yet it challenges the market leader. Its product is hardly new, although some flavours may be. Its promotion strategy is different from most. The case study crosses the boundaries between this and the next Enquiry.

Open Question

Is it ethical to promote one's product on ethical grounds?

Peace, love and ice cream

L AST week saw the arrival of a new player in the 'superpremium' market – rich, flavoursome, but highly fattening ice-cream sold at fancy prices – hitherto dominated by Häagen-Dazs.

Although the Grand Metropolitan operation with the unpronounceable name and notoriously sensual advertisements is the main target for Ben & Jerry's, it is not inconceivable that the US company could win customers who have so far failed to lap up a product that puts the traditional vanilla block in the shade.

For, while Häagen-Dazs could be said to sell sex with its ice cream, Ben & Jerry's identifies its product with 'peace and understanding'.

In the United States, where its sales of more than $130m (now £87m) in 1992 gave it 40 per cent of the luxury ice cream market (Häagen-Dazs has just about all the rest), the New England-based company distributes 7.5 per cent of pre-tax profits (nearly $1m in 1992) to charities through its Ben & Jerry Foundation.

It also campaigns on a range of social and environmental issues and obtains its dairy supplies – at premium prices – from family-run farms and co-operatives.

Indeed, in 1992 – when tough economic conditions might have been expected to make life difficult for a luxury product – sales grew by an unprecedented 36 per cent. And with demand outstripping supply, Ben & Jerry's has been able to commission a new plant – which will provide the capacity for expansion into the UK and other parts of Europe.

The company already has a joint venture in the former Soviet Union – conceived as a step towards greater understanding before the end of the Cold War – and a licensee in Israel. Having expanded throughout the US largely through franchising, it is on the lookout for like-minded companies in order to assist in its international growth.

While some who are wedded to good causes can put off supporters, Ben & Jerry's seems to win fans through a light-hearted approach. It has long sponsored film and music festivals, and its Waterbury factory has become Vermont's most popular tourist spot. Inside the factories, teams of workers known as 'joy gangs' organise pranks and jollity to brighten the working day.

But there are more positive, and potentially far-reaching, effects of the policy. For instance, nobody in the company – including the founders, who are still on salary – is paid more than seven times as much as the lowest paid.

While this is seen as a good motivator for the more junior employees, it has been regarded as a bar to recruiting top-level executives. Mr Cohen prefers to see it as a way of 'pre-screening' applicants. It reduces the size of the pool, but makes it more likely that applicants will share the company's values, he says.

Equally, the 1992 annual report included – for the fifth time – a comprehensive 'social assessment' by an independent consultant that looked at such issues as treatment of employees and effects on the local community and the environment. It was generally complimentary of the company, which claims never to have made staff redundant – at slack times, employees are kept on the pay-roll and seconded to local not-for-profit projects.

But Mr Cohen is not satisfied. Believing that the organisation has achieved much in recruiting women to senior positions, he is anxious that Ben & Jerry's – even though it is located in a rural part of the north-east with few minorities – should better represent the people it is selling to.

One initiative demonstrates its unusual approach. Having pledged last year to examine some of the processes that its workers were required to carry out, it has stopped making one of its best-known products because it could not find a safer way of doing it.

There were protests from customers about the disappearance of the 'brownie ice cream sandwich'. But, according to Mr Cohen, until there is a machine to replace the repetitive motion that threatens to injure operators' arms, continuing production is 'not an option'.

Source: Adapted from the *Independent on Sunday*, 3 April 1994

Enquiry 3: What powers do consumers have?

Scope

Consumers' welfare is greatly affected by what businesses do. Equally, through market forces consumers can have a substantial influence on business. Also, through combining together as pressure groups, consumers can influence both businesses and governments.

Some business decisions have an adverse affect on society as a whole, especially when there are negative externalities, spillover effects which damage the environment. Other decisions may have a favourable effect. Both as consumers and as members of the wider society, people wish to influence what happens in business.

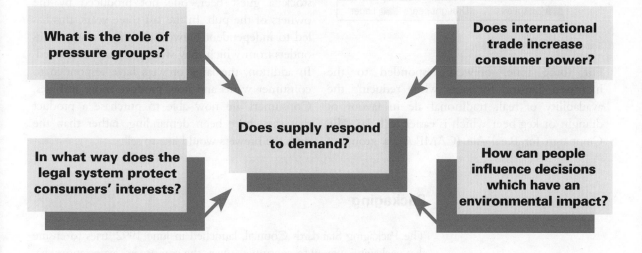

What is the role of pressure groups?

Does international trade increase consumer power?

Does supply respond to demand?

In what way does the legal system protect consumers' interests?

How can people influence decisions which have an environmental impact?

Opening evidence

Campaign for Real Ale

The beer market can be divided into three sectors: cask-conditioned ales (usually known as real ale), lagers and draught beers. The consumer (aided by government legislation) has been able to exert some influence.

Source: Campaign for Real Ale

For some time, brewers responded to the increased demand for lager while reducing the availability of real, traditional ale in favour of draught or keg beer which is easier to keep. The Campaign for Real Ale (CAMRA), a group of real ale enthusiasts, saw the decline in the availability of their kind of beer. They produced the *Good Beer Guide* which identified pubs where real ale was sold. Once people knew where to find it, demand grew. Twenty-one years later, CAMRA still tries to help consumers to get the product they want. The brewers, realising that there is a sizeable market of people who will look for well-kept real ale, are providing it in many more pubs.

Perhaps more significantly, the Monopolies and Mergers Commission ruling on large brewers has also had an effect. Pub tenants are now allowed to stock a guest beer, one not produced by the owners of the pub. In the last three years, this has led to independent brewers gaining access to sales outlets from which they were previously excluded. In addition, the large brewers have responded to consumer wants and now produce more real ales. Consumers are now able to purchase a product that they have been demanding, rather than the ones the brewers would like to sell.

Packaging

The Packaging Standards Council, launched in June 1992, tries to ensure that packaging offered to consumers meets the consumers' expectations, has a minimum impact on the environment and is continuously improving. The Council, an independent organisation, is funded by industry and attempts to put pressure on manufacturers. In a recent case, a complaint about excess packaging of Sainsbury's pitta bread was investigated. The company view was that the two layers of packaging were necessary to protect the product while in transit. Recognising that other supermarkets make do with only one layer of packaging, Sainsbury had a trial period of using one layer and has been able to keep this arrangement as permanent. This is a small gain for the environment but a success for a small pressure group that works exclusively with producers after receiving consumers' complaints.

Windfarms

... so we went for a walk on the moors. It was a beautiful day. As we neared the top, walking over the crest of the hill, a windfarm came into view. 'How do you feel about that?' I said.

'Well, we don't like it, none of us do. Even when we're inside the house, we can hear it humming, the whole time. We've written to our MP but I don't suppose it will make any difference.'

I thought to myself that it's a real eyesore and spoils the scenery for miles around. But then, I'm a member of Friends of the Earth and they are in favour of clean, renewable energy sources. Windfarms are clean and the energy is renewable. Shouldn't I be in favour of this? I don't know what to think ...

In search of quality

In July 1991 the *Citizen's Charter* was published. Its objectives were to improve the quality of public service provision in the UK and to assure the rights of the users of these services.

The government envisages the attainment of these objectives through a combination of the following:

■ more privatisation
■ wider competition
■ further contracting out
■ more performance-related pay
■ published national and local targets
■ comprehensive publication of information on standards obtained
■ more effective complaints procedures
■ enhanced independent inspection
■ enhanced redress for the citizen for service failures.

British Rail

In 1992 the *Passenger's Charter* was introduced, setting out punctuality and reliability standards for services within Network South-East. If, on average over the previous 12 months, either punctuality has been 3% below target or reliability more than 1% below target, passengers holding season or monthly tickets will obtain a 5% discount when they renew their tickets.

Examples of targets		Objective	Performance 1990–91	% 1991–92
Punctuality:	within 5 minutes urban	90	90	92
Reliability:	urban at least	99	97.1	98.4
Train enquiries:	% of calls answered in 30 secs	95	78.5	86.6
Ticket offices:	peak-time queuing	5 min.	100	100
Carriage clean:	interior daily wash	100	91	95

Source: Adapted from *Accounting Technician*, March 1993

1 Consumer sovereignty

In a *laissez-faire* economy the allocation of resources is determined by market forces which reflect sellers' inclination to supply and buyers' demand. Preceding Enquiries looked at how sellers can use their power to influence and control market forces. This Enquiry considers the power of the buyers.

Harley Davidson

The Harley Davidson Motor Bike Company sells 1000cc-plus motorbikes. It is very well established in the USA and did not feel at all under threat from the early introduction of Japanese motor bikes. Honda, Suzuki, etc. started to sell their small bikes in the US market and began to gain acceptance for their reliable machines. By the time Harley Davidson noticed, the Japanese companies were selling large bikes in direct competition and the US manufacturers were losing the battle for market share. By not recognising that the Japanese companies were satisfying consumer demand, Harley Davidson was losing its own business. It was staying with a standard well-established product rather than addressing the market. This has now changed, the company has become much more market oriented and produces bikes that are in competition with the smaller Japanese models (as well as the more famous larger bikes). A major turnaround in company performance has been achieved.

Adam Smith's *The Wealth of Nations* (1776) is often quoted as the economics text that first explained the role of the market in bringing buyers and sellers together. The invisible hand works to allocate resources in line with consumer demand. There are many buyers and sellers, which ensures that no one person is important enough in the market to manipulate the price. Thus the price will be kept down by competition, at a level which reflects the true opportunity cost of the resources used in production.

Consumer sovereignty

In practice, many markets are very different from this. In previous Enquiries it has become clear that there may not be many sellers. They can have influence over the market and can disadvantage the customers in terms of both a higher price and reduced choice.

Consumer-led markets

In an ideal world, buyers would be powerful enough to influence producers to supply the goods and services that they want. In a consumer-led economy, the producers have to respond to the wishes of the buyers in order to make a profit. In such a scenario consumers are sovereign and their wishes take precedence over the suppliers' wishes.

Figure 3.1 Consumer demand and business success

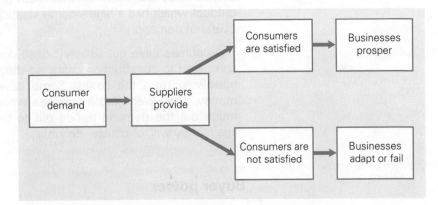

Supply and demand

An increase in consumer demand for a particular product will mean that prices will rise. Producers will find that product more profitable. These profits will attract new entrants to the industry. Resources will move into production of the desirable product. As they do, competition will intensify and the price will be driven back down to the level at which it just covers the average total cost of production. Similarly, if consumer demand for a product falls, the price will fall and losses will be made. In time producers will adjust by reducing output or going out of business altogether and the supply will again match demand at a price which reflects production costs.

In theory, therefore, suppliers have to respond to the demands of the consumers in order to stay in business. This implies that consumers have *all* the power in a market. Clearly, this is not the case. Suppliers have considerable scope to mould consumers' preferences and to control what is made available to them. However, in recent years competition among producers has sometimes led to the development of a much more market-oriented approach. When this happens, suppliers are acknowledging the force of consumer demand.

Golf courses

Rising demand for golf courses has been quite good for job creation, attracting considerable resources into the business. On average, golfers spend over £1,000 a year on their enthusiasm. A large golf course can employ 50 people.

Unfortunately, the golf promoters overdid it during the late 1980s. They invested in a large number of new courses. Some of these turned out to be quite challenging for beginner players, who didn't want to pay high fees to play on courses where they were continually in difficulties. Then, when the early 1990s recession arrived, they cut back on their activities to save money. With a product which had a high income elasticity of demand, capacity had overshot demand.

The courses have not usually closed down. Running costs are low compared to construction costs, so they have kept going, often by borrowing from the banks. Some developers have lost a lot of money. They went into a business where rising demand promised much but the demand turned out to be unreliable. If it increases again, they will, of course, do well.

Buyer power

The buyer in the market place is sometimes more powerful than the seller. This could be the case when a large organisation is buying components from small producers. It can also occur if a retail outlet is buying the produce of a small manufacturer, with a view to reselling these goods to the public. Another example might be where a well-known retailer is negotiating the cost of setting up a new store within an out-of-town shopping centre.

If, in a particular market, there is only one person or organisation buying the product or service, the situation is called a **monopsony**. This is unusual, but sometimes there is very little choice as to buyers. A train driver can sell his or her services only to BR. Similarly, for a nuclear physicist there are few potential employers.

The above examples are not pure monopsonies as the sellers of these services do have other choices. These may be very limited if they wish to use their specialist skills but alternatives do exist. The availability of alternatives defines the extent to which any market is controlled by a monopsony purchaser.

Consumer needs and wants

Consumer wants are unlimited. Although there are individuals who deliberately choose modest life-styles, society as a whole is far from having achieved all that people want in material terms.

One of the tasks of any business, and of the marketing department in particular, is to turn consumers' wants into a demand for the company's products. If the company can successfully engineer this transformation from wants to demand, the business is likely to succeed. At each stage in progressing from wants to demand to profits, the marketing department can become involved.

Figure 3.2 Transforming consumer wants

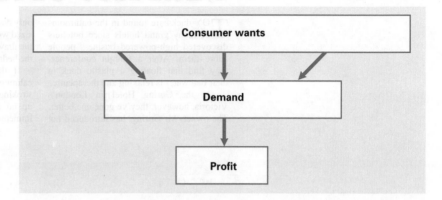

For a marketing department there are three stages, which apply to all products, in trying to transform the wants or demands of consumers into profits for the business. These stages are:

1 Investigating – to discover what the consumer wants or if there are needs that have not been met.
2 Designing – to develop a product or service that meets these identified needs.
3 Selling – devising ways to persuade the consumer to buy the newly designed product.

In reality, this does not always seem to happen. There may be products on the market that do not meet the demands of individuals. (Does anyone really need an electric carving knife?) Usually if this happens the products remain unsold and the company will withdraw the goods or repackage them. Because the UK is a market-driven economy, unwanted goods cannot remain on the market for very long.

In the example quoted of the electric carving knife, it may appear at first glance that no one would buy the good but this fails to take account of the highly segmented market in a developed economy. Some people with disabilities and some elderly people greatly value an electric carving knife. Marketing strategies need to be backed up by a genuine knowledge of the true nature of the market. But how did hoteliers discover the marketing power of plastic ducks (see case study on p. 60)?

Market segmentation

The complex balance between consumer sovereignty and marketing strategies is different for every product. Genuine attempts to meet consumer demand increase consumer influence. Marketing strategies which attempt to reduce competition can reduce consumer choice and limit consumer influence in the market place.

Market orientation

TOY ducks are found in the bathrooms of many grand hotels since hoteliers discovered high-powered business people adore them. After a fraught conference, they find that floating a plastic duck in their bathwater is relaxing and therapeutic.

At the Goring Hotel in London's Victoria, however, they've gone one better. The owner, Mr Goring, has introduced not only ducks but extremely real-looking, full-sized woolly sheep. They recline in front of the drawing room fire and stand in many of the bedrooms.

I don't know why, but they are a calming, heart-lifting, joyous sight. And stroking them on a fraught day cheered me up no end. Mr Major ought to buy one immediately.

Source: *Daily Mail*, 12 January 1994

International trade

Imports often provide a much larger choice for the consumer than would be available from the domestic market. This enables consumers to match their wants in the market place more precisely. Measures such as the GATT Uruguay round of trade negotiations, which facilitate trade, tend to increase consumer power. Imports from a wider range of producers will become possible and competition will therefore tend to increase. This will make prices keener and perhaps also make for improvements in product quality.

Open Question

In what ways does buying imports make consumers better off?

2 Consumer power and pressure groups

Consumer pressure

In May 1994, *Which?* magazine published tests on fridges, trainers, hot-air guns and paint strippers. In each case it identified best buys and pointed out any particular failings of individual products. It also included articles examining the safety of the Channel Tunnel, the possible pitfalls of buying at car boot sales and problems with cash machines. Over time, the magazine covers all aspects of consumer interest.

Consumer tests and publications, such as *Which?*, have made it much more difficult for producers to get away with design faults, unreliable products and any other failure to take account of the safety and convenience of the buyer or user. Over the past two decades, firms have become sensitive to the results of consumer tests and the general level of safety and reliability has improved. Firms have much to lose from an adverse report. Consumers can save considerable trouble and expense by making sure that they are well informed before they buy.

The *media* have been effective in publicising the effects of certain drugs. Starting in the 1960s, when the effect of thalidomide on unborn children was widely reported, there have been a number of frequently prescribed drugs with serious side effects which have eventually been withdrawn or used much more sparingly because of press publicity. The addictive nature of tranquillisers was exposed rather before doctors became significantly more cautious in prescribing them.

Mary Whitehouse was able to exert considerable influence on the nature of TV broadcasting by campaigning against explicit sexual material being shown. Using the media with skill, she mobilised an element of public opinion, creating a pressure group which represented traditional family-oriented views to the broadcasting authorities.

ASH has consistently represented the views of non-smokers. It has worked to publicise the health risks inherent in tobacco smoking and to bring pressure to bear to reduce smoking in public places and in restaurants. Although, initially, it appeared that the power of the tobacco industry to advertise was enormous, this has been steadily eroded as governments have responded to the anti-smoking lobby.

US feminists have collectively campaigned against pornographic magazines being openly displayed in news stands. Although the magazines are still on sale, their presence is less obvious.

Greenpeace sends highly trained people to disrupt the creation of environmentally questionable structures. While the effect is likely to be temporary, the resulting publicity raises awareness of Greenpeace's views.

Pressure groups exist to try to influence various sectors of society. They may be aimed at people or they may try to exert pressure on companies or the government. The basic principle underlying any pressure group is that by combining, otherwise weak individuals may have much more impact and influence. Some pressure groups are more involved in moral issues than in the market place, but many do exist to influence what happens in the market economy.

There are three main types of pressure groups:

1 Protective groups look after the interests of their own members and try to exert pressure only in their interests e.g. the RAC, trade unions and professional associations.
2 Promotional groups try to influence the public at large. These can work at a national or local level. Examples include the RSPCA, Respect for Animals (formed from Lynx), World Wide Fund for Nature.

3 Ad hoc groups take on the role of a pressure group to publicise a particular cause. For example, Sunday trading was supported by the DIY stores but opposed by the Keep Sunday Special Group, while in France this same theme was taken up by Virgin Megastores.

Open Question

What other pressure groups'
activities are important
to consumers?

In terms of its effect on the power of the consumer, the Consumers' Association has had considerable impact. It exerts pressure on businesses to keep their products safe, reliable and fairly priced. It also lobbies the government to ensure that the legal system gives due weight to the interests of the consumer. By giving its 800,000 members extensive information on numerous products, it enables consumers to make much more informed choices.

The role of the lobbyist

Pressure groups try to readjust the balance of power within any market. In theory, the pressure group is trying to look after the weaker player in any market situation; a large number of people will join together to act as a united group. In reality, pressure groups are just as likely to be used by businesses to help them get their own way and protect them from legislation which is to their disadvantage. When a pressure group works on politicians it is said to *lobby* Parliament in pursuit of its objectives.

Forum of Private Businesses

Small businesses are often at the mercy of their debtors when they try to ensure that their cash flow is sufficient to pay their own creditors. Many businesses faced bankruptcy in the 1990s because they could not collect the money that was owed to them. In 1993 the size of the debtors' bill owed to small businesses in the UK was £50 billion (compared to £44 billion owed to banks by small businesses). In many cases the problem arises because a large organisation is slow to pay its suppliers and this has a knock-on effect through subcontractors and smaller businesses.

On average, small businesses wait 81 days for payment after they have sent an invoice so, obviously, the voluntary code between businesses does not work. There is also very little opportunity to seek legal remedy because of the costs involved, the time taken and the damage to good will. The Forum of Private Businesses, which represents 21,000 members, claims that the problem is much worse in the UK than in the rest of Europe. Their solution has been to prepare a draft parliamentary bill allowing companies to charge interest on the money that is owed. This lobby group will try to get their ideas accepted by the government and introduced as law. This could be as part of the Budget, as a private members bill or as part of other legislation.

3 Consumers, society and the environment

Rising consumer spending may be desired by many people but it does have environmental implications. When the environment deteriorates, society suffers as a whole, so society is as much a stakeholder in business decisions as the consumer. The 'environment lobby' expresses the concerns of the many people who are personally worried about the environmental impact of economic development.

The Cardiff barrage

Early in 1994, the European Commission told the UK government that work on constructing the Cardiff barrage could not start until assurances had been given that there would be measures to compensate birds for loss of habitat there.

The barrage is designed to create a freshwater lake where previously there were mudflats. This should stimulate development along the waterfront. The EU Environment Commissioner said that the development would be acceptable but only if the birds are provided with alternative habitats. This could be done by classifying the rest of the Severn estuary as a special protection area and also making a national conservation plan for dunlins and redshanks.

The Department of the Environment had hoped to keep the correspondence confidential but a letter from the Commission was leaked to Friends of the Earth, who reported it to the newspapers. Friends of the Earth said the UK had one of the worst records in Europe for creating special protection areas.

Many pressure groups are concerned with environmental issues. This is a reflection of the interests of individuals within the Western economies in the 1990s. People who are strongly interested in current environmental issues do join pressure groups. However, there is also a much larger group of people – consumers – who are concerned enough to alter their buying habits and cut down on consumption of environmentally unfriendly products. The existence of this group has caused some producers to give much more attention to the environmental impact of their products. However, the effectiveness of this trend is greatly dependent upon consumers having good information and this, in turn, depends very much on the activity of pressure groups and the media. It also depends upon producers not making phoney improvements and advertising them as a real increase in environmental friendliness.

Although many consumers think that resources are wasted in packaging which then creates more waste, the UK government has not yet taken any action over the excess packaging of products. Nor has it implemented any controls over the recycling of packaging materials. The government's Advisory Committee on the Environment, set up in 1991, has suggested that the UK should introduce recycling policies, although the committee recognises that industry does not have the capacity to cope with a large influx of material that needs to be recycled. This situation contrasts with the legislation introduced in other European countries where strict controls exist.

There are genuine anxieties about the cost of recycling, which is often higher in current money terms than the cost of throwing things away. The difficulty is that the long-term costs of environmental degradation are very unclear; they may be very high but it is hard to tell how they compare with the costs of recycling.

German ambitions on recycling

In Germany, the system of proportional representation is kinder to small political parties than the UK 'first past the post' system. The Green Party has had some electoral successes and these have allowed it to bring pressure to bear on governments. The result has been a considerable amount of environmental legislation.

The 'Green Point' scheme ensures that any packaging that has a green circle on it must be recycled. In addition, the shop selling the product must make arrangements for this recycling and provide collection points at the place of purchase. Failure to provide for recycling, or failure by consumers to recycle, leads to heavy fines.

Figure 3.3 German recycling plans for 1993

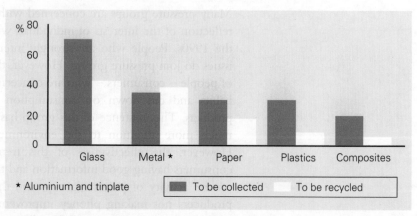

Source: Environment Council

Figure 3.3 shows how one European country is trying to tackle the recycling problem, placing responsibility on business to sort out their own packaging. In the UK some supermarkets are making plans for a similar scheme, with the provision of bottle banks, paper banks, plastic and can collecting areas, etc.

Not all the waste disposed of in the UK is the responsibility of the supermarkets and retailers. In fact, packaging makes up a surprisingly small amount of the average dustbin's content, as shown in Figure 3.4.

Figure 3.4 Contents of the average UK dustbin (%)

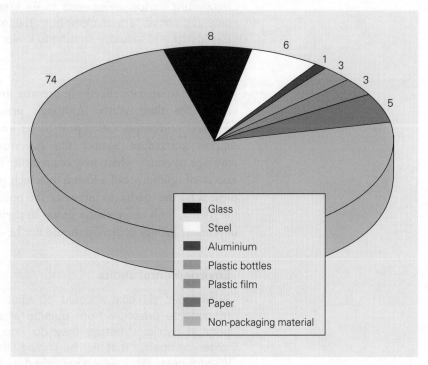

Source: Adapted from the *Guardian*, 30 October 1993

Late in 1993 the EU agreed on what to do about packaging: countries should aim to recover 50–65% of all packaging materials. By the year 2000, a minimum of 25% and a maximum of 45% should be recycled. This is less stringent than the laws of Germany and the Netherlands, but more so than most other countries.

Getting some response

Responding to pressure!

The EU imposes limits on the number of pollutants allowed within the air. The problems with ozone and high concentrations of nitrogen oxide and hydrocarbons are encouraging both governments and local authorities to look at their policies on transport. Some cities have responded by reducing the amount of traffic allowed into the city (Florence), some have introduced taxes for driving into the city (Oslo) and some have experimented with charging meters (Cambridge). The German local government of Baden-Württemberg is the latest to restrict the type of traffic allowed in the cities and towns within its region. If, at the end of each month, the pollution is considered to be excessive, the local government of Baden-Württemberg will introduce four days of controls. These involve maximum motorway speeds of 64 kmph (40 mph), only cars with catalytic converters or clean-burn diesel engines being allowed into the towns and industry shifting to lower levels of production.

If they are to operate effectively, pressure groups need to use the media as a vehicle for their views. Although privately owned newspapers and television companies can appear to be interested only in profit, they do support campaigns against the government and provide immediate coverage of events which may discredit it. They also provide an outlet for a variety of opinions and a forum in which politicians can air their views. In these ways the media do influence the political system. The importance of the media, both as a pressure group in itself and as a channel for the views of pressure groups generally, should not be underestimated.

Environmental audits

Businesses do take account of what their customers want; they respond to pressure from outside and listen to the views of the general public. Whether they do *enough* is another matter. One large company that is beginning to respond is the National Westminster Bank which published its first *Environmental Report* in 1993. It commented:

'We recognise that the pursuit of economic growth and a healthy environment must be closely linked and that ecological protection and sustainable development are collective responsibilities in which governments, businesses, individuals and communities all have a role to play' (part of the Environmental Policy Statement in July 1993). The report goes on to highlight some of the adjustments that had occurred in the past year. Some of these specific changes have included:

- 15% of the car fleet is now diesel-engined
- energy saving in 1992 was 8.76%
- use of recycled paper for envelopes and customer statements
- reduction in the volume of paper used
- adhering to building design standards.

The policy of being aware about responsibility for the environment is being driven by the board of the bank and, in the report, the Chairman commented: 'Business should be increasingly conscious that it must become part of the environmental solution, effecting the necessary changes in the industrial cycle to underpin sustainable development. For all of us as individuals the word "environment" has acquired a conceptual value and a power it did not have before. The reasons for our concerns stem from an analysis based upon today's knowledge of yesterday's action. The acknowledged need is to switch from this use of hindsight to the application of foresight in environmental matters.'

4 Consumer rights

The consumer often has very little power or influence when compared with a business and sometimes it is necessary for a helping hand to be given, in the form of some protection from government. The law recognises that it is necessary to grant certain rights to the consumer and some responsibilities to businesses, in an attempt to redress the balance between individuals and firms.

Contract law

A contract is simply an agreement that is enforceable by law and is the main way in which people do business. This enables markets to function properly. Whenever consumers purchase products, or businesses arrange a sale, they are entering into a legally binding contract. Although this happens millions of times every day, a set number of procedures must occur to ensure that a contract exists between both parties. For a contract to be in existence, the following events must occur:

1 An 'offer' is made.
2 This offer is 'accepted'.
3 Each party to the contract provides 'consideration'.

For example, someone may offer a car for sale at £5,000 and someone else will accept the offer. Both sides give up something in this arrangement (£5,000 or the car) and, as such, each provides consideration. If these three events occur, assuming both parties intend to make and are able to make a contract, both sides will be legally responsible for their part of the bargain. If one side then decides not to honour their commitment, there is a **breach of contract** and legal remedies are available for the other party. The court decides what happens next.

There are three possible remedies:

1 Damages – where a sum of money is paid as compensation.
2 Specific performance – where the offender is ordered to complete their part of the contract.
3 Injunction – where the offender is prevented from doing something.

In addition to the legal remedies available in the event of a broken contract, there is a range of legislation aimed at protecting the consumer. These laws are considered necessary because of the unequal balance of power each side brings to the contract. Although few contracts end up being disputed in the courts, the existence of the law means that the vast majority of contracts are made in accordance with it.

Consumer protection legislation

The Sale of Goods Act 1979 – gives consumers purchasing goods from a retailer some rights in the event of the goods not being of a suitable quality. The customer is entitled to have a refund if the goods are:

1 not as described
2 not of merchantable (satisfactory) quality
3 not fit for the purpose for which they were intended to be used.

These conditions do not give consumers the right to return something they do not like, but they do ensure that the customer receives the goods that have been paid for. These rights do not apply in a private sale.

The Trade Descriptions Act 1968 – gives consumers protection against traders who mislead by applying a wrong description of goods for sale. If the seller makes a statement that cannot be checked and that may or may not be true, it does not count as a description, e.g. 'This car is a good little number'. Statements of opinion and mere puffs do not count, e.g. 'I think this is a very reliable car' or 'The best car dealership in town'. In the event of a consumer suffering from a false description of goods which caused him or her to purchase the goods, there is a remedy in the criminal courts.

The Unfair Contract Terms Act 1977 – contracts between buyers and sellers are often thought to benefit the seller because of their greater bargaining power. To prevent sellers adding lots of clauses in contracts that will disadvantage the consumer, the Unfair Contract Terms Act attempts to redress the balance. Suppliers are not allowed to introduce clauses that will take away consumers' statutory rights nor can they limit their liability for personal injury or death, unless those clauses can be shown to be reasonable.

The Consumer Protection Act 1987 – sometimes consumers are injured as a result of faulty products. This act aims to ensure that producers insure their product against its potential for causing harm to consumers. The Act imposes liability for defective products on the producers; it cannot be avoided. This allows users of the product, even if they did not purchase it, to sue the manufacturer.

The Consumer Credit Act 1984 – ensures that the consumer is given adequate information about the financial responsibilities being undertaken before the contract is arranged. The lender is required to make available details about the annual percentage rate of interest (APR), the deposit needed, the cash price, the total credit price and details about the right to cancel the arrangement.

The Food Safety Act 1990 – under this Act it is an offence for a person to render food injurious to health with the intent that it shall be sold for human consumption. This wide-ranging description means that anyone who prepares food or processes ingredients has a responsibility to take care. To enforce this Act, officers have the power to inspect food which is for sale, has been sold or is in the process of preparation.

The Trading Standards Department – many industries have an ombudsman who is there to investigate disputes between individuals and companies within the industry. They are all independent and offer impartial advice to customers. Their powers are restricted but they are usually able to act much faster than if the case were taken to the courts. Their approach is informal and, if they are not able to investigate on a person's behalf, they will offer advice on how they can proceed.

The Insurance Ombudsman

This free service attempts to solve disputes between individuals and their insurance companies. If an individual is unable to resolve a disagreement with the company concerned, the Insurance Ombudsman will intervene. If the case cannot be settled by bringing the two sides together, the Ombudsman will make a common sense decision based on the law and good insurance practice. In these circumstances an individual can accept the decision and receive compensation or reject the decision and take other action against the company, which can include legal action. In this sense the Ombudsman does not reduce the individual's rights but provides a quicker, more direct route to solving problems.

The Citizen's Charter

In July 1991 the Prime Minister presented to Parliament a White Paper entitled *The Citizen's Charter*. This has become a government initiative aimed at raising standards in the delivery of public services, at both local and national level. The White Paper had four main themes:

1 Quality – new programmes for improving the quality of public service.
2 Choice - providing consumer choice wherever possible as a spur to quality management.
3 Standards – to provide the individual with service standards and permitting individual action where these standards are unacceptable.
4 Value – since the individual citizen is a taxpayer, public services must provide value for money.

Many public sector organisations have followed the Conservative Government's initiative on charters and introduced their own standards. The value of *The Citizen's Charter* is not entirely clear. It can be argued that it has raised consumers' expectations about standards and encouraged the public to complain, something the British are not very good at doing. Some say that the public sector organisations with charters do not like having to deal with these complaints and are therefore trying to prevent them by offering a good service. Other people have not been so generous. They have described the charter initiative as a waste of time because no financial compensation is available to consumers if things go wrong. Without this, there is no real incentive for the public sector to improve its performance. It remains to be seen whether improvements turn out to be real and sustained.

Regulation

In some markets, regulation is used to protect the consumer. For example, the Civil Aviation Authority controls airline ticket sales. It makes tough rules for travel agents selling discounted tickets or cheap holidays. They have to have a licence unless they provide a flight or a guaranteed refund. The objective is to prevent travellers from being stranded abroad. Tour operators who take out a licence contribute to a fund which is used to pay for return fares in the event of the operator going bankrupt. This is just one example of regulation.

5 Consumer power or consumer preferences

Consumer sovereignty can end in creating an allocation of resources which consumers dislike in practice. Individual decisions, made in each person's own interest, can destroy some of the quality of life. Nowhere is this more evident than in the debate about road transport.

Car crazy

NOTHING must be allowed to obstruct the forward march of 'the great car economy', Margaret Thatcher declared soon after reaching Downing Street in 1979. She was as good as her word. Millions of her fellow citizens, prompted by soaring rail fares and deteriorating public transport, also took to the roads. Lady Thatcher's worship of the car has contributed to Britain having some of the most congested roads and poorest-performing railways in Western Europe.

Fifteen years and nine transport ministers later, her successors in government are still searching for a coherent transport strategy. A review of the government's 20-year road-building programme now means that plans to carve new motorways through open countryside will be abandoned and new radical highways into inner cities will be scrapped. Instead, priority will be given to widening existing motorways, shortening planning procedures and accelerating new bypasses.

These changes are an acknowledgement of the growing public resistance to new roads, but they do nothing to address the vacuum in policy. Confronted by voters' irritation with the inadequacy of both roads and public transport, ministers are facing in several directions. The Department of Transport is pushing ahead with huge extensions to the heavily congested M25, while the Department of the Environment is alarmed by the projected growth in road traffic.

The need for a sustainable transport strategy is urgent. According to forecasts by the Department of Transport, traffic on all roads will double over the next three decades. Already Britain's roads have almost twice as many cars for the available road space as France or Belgium. And the British rely on their cars more than anyone else in Europe except the French (see Figures 3.5 and 3.6). Even road lobbyists accept that continuing to allow the great car economy to roar on would require large swatches of the countryside to be covered in concrete. The situation is particularly acute in cities. In 1991 a study by the Department of Transport concluded that 'town centres simply cannot take unrestricted traffic growth ... And there is no point in increasing the capacity of roads leading into areas which are already congested'. A study by the Confederation of British Industry claims that traffic congestion adds £15 billion annually to the nation's industrial costs.

Confronted by this dilemma of soaring demand and restricted supply, ministers know that cars

Figure 3.5 Car kilometres per unit of wealth

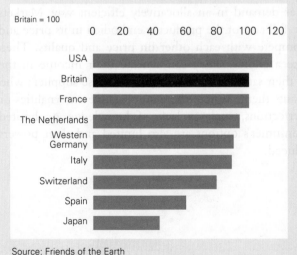

Source: Friends of the Earth

Figure 3.6 Road traffic

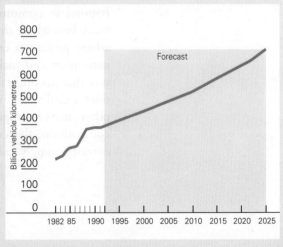

Source: Department of Transport

and lorries will have to be restrained by either price or regulation, but they are afraid of incurring the wrath of drivers by doing either. Letting congestion exert its own costly discipline is seen by many as the easiest option. Unfortunately, doing nothing, allied to a tax system which positively encourages the use of cars, has merely aggravated the problem. Drivers have high fixed costs in insurance, licence fees and capital depreciation, but the additional running cost of using their car, mainly fuel, is relatively small. On most journeys, rail is rarely competitive on price. For example, a standard return rail fare to Oxford from London is £25.10, four times as much as the fuel costs of a car able to carry five passengers.

Source: Adapted from *The Economist*, 12 March 1994

Queuing for the train.

Open Question

How can consumer preferences influence transport policy?

The dilemma here is that the government is faced with a trade-off between raising the cost of motoring and accepting increased environmental damage. Consumers who make use of their own private transport are unlikely to welcome increased fuel taxes or road pricing, even though they deplore the environmental problems. There is no real public consensus on the problem and, for the most part, people have not yet appreciated the gravity of the trade-off which exists. The government is unwilling to pursue a policy which might be unpopular with many voters. There is thus a lack of resolution in society's approach to the problem.

Where there are negative externalities, the market, left to itself, may not respond to consumer demand in an allocatively efficient way. Markets work best where the full cost of the product is embodied in its price and where producers compete with each other on price and quality. Then consumers can make a choice. They can allocate their income in the way that maximises their satisfaction and they can choose suppliers who offer a deal which suits them. Where there are negative externalities or other market imperfections, such as lack of knowledge or limited competition, the consumer's options are also limited and their powers correspondingly reduced.

Enquiry 4: What is the market power of stakeholders?

Scope

In any business there are a number of stakeholders. These are people who have an interest in the activities of the business because they are themselves involved in it in some way. Consumers and society as a whole are all stakeholders and their involvement was discussed in Enquiry 3. Within the business, the important stakeholders are the employees, the managers and the shareholders. Each enjoys an element of market power, much constrained by the power of each other and of the legal framework. The nature of each group's interest is different. Inevitably therefore, there are times when these interests conflict with each other.

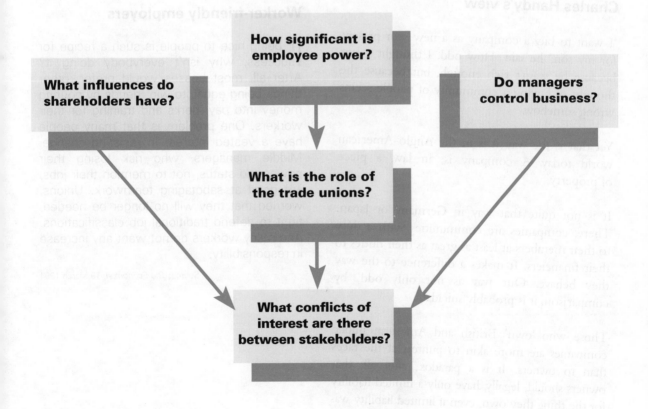

Opening evidence

Annual general meetings

WHAT is the point of annual meetings? In America and Britain big shareholders rarely bother to attend, leaving small investors to eat the free lunch with top managers. In Germany big shareholders put in an appearance at the lengthy meetings, but little that is controversial is said. In France meetings are brief and poorly attended, even though some firms pay shareholders a small fee if they turn

up. Yet annual meetings take up lots of management time and cost a fortune to stage.

Source: *The Economist*, 12 March 1994

Charles Handy's view

'I want to buy a company as a new year present for my son,' he said. How odd, I thought – not because he wasn't rich enough, but because the thought of buying a community of people seems wrong somehow.

Yet that is the way it is in the Anglo–American world today. A company is, in law, a piece of property.

It is not quite that way in Germany or Japan. There, companies are communities with a duty to their members at least as great as their duties to their financiers. It makes a difference to the way they behave. Our way is not only odd, by comparison, it is probably suicidal.

Those who 'own' British and American public companies are more akin to punters at the races than to owners. It is a paradox, after all, that owners should, legally, have only a limited liability for the thing they own, even if limited liability was the spark that set the industrial revolution alight.

Source: Charles Handy

Worker-friendly employers

IF being nice to people is such a recipe for success, why isn't everybody doing it? After all, most bosses would prefer, other things being equal, to win friends by pouring money into pay, perks and training for their workers. One problem is that many people have a vested interest in resisting change. Middle managers, who risk losing their power and status, not to mention their jobs, are good at sabotaging teamwork. Unions, worried that they will no longer be needed, fight to defend traditional job classifications. And many workers do not want any increase in responsibility.

Source: *The Economist*, 19 March 1994

The social chapter

The Maastricht Summit of December 1991 decided to adopt the social chapter within the European Community from 1993. The UK negotiated an opt-out clause and therefore does not have to introduce these social policy initiatives which are binding on all the other eleven countries of the EU. Some of the main contents of the social chapter are:

1 Freedom of movement within Europe.
2 The right of all EU nationals to receive equal treatment as nationals of the host nation.
3 All employment is to be 'fairly remunerated'.
4 The establishment of controls on the organisation and flexibility of working time, including a maximum working week.
5 Protection for employees engaged in other than full-time jobs of indefinite duration (part-timers, temporary workers, shift-workers, etc.).
6 The right to annual leave and a weekly rest period.
7 Every EU citizen to have 'adequate social protection'.
8 The right to a 'minimum income' for all workers excluded from the labour market without being able to claim unemployment benefit.
9 The right of employees to belong to any professional organisation or trade union.
10 The freedom to negotiate and conclude collective agreements.
11 The right to take collective action, e.g. to strike.
12 Equal treatment for men and women.
13 Further developments to ensure satisfactory health and safety conditions at work, including a movement to standardise these in the EU.
14 A minimum age of employment of 16.
15 The right of young workers to vocational training for at least two years.

The social chapter has proved to be contentious with many British politicians and many have spoken against this agreement.

Pay and status

Salaries for sales assistants in Boots, outside London

May 1992	£6,162–7,703
July 1993	£6,841–8,551

Source: IDS Pay Directory

Boots' Chief Executive's salary

March 1991	£343,000	including a £6,000 bonus
March 1992	£571,000	including a £186,000 bonus
March 1993	£615,000	

Boots dividends

March 1991–1992	12.4p per share
March 1992–1993	13.4p per share

Source: Boots, Annual Report and Accounts, 1993

For comparison: inflation in the year to March 1992, 4.1%; to March 1993, 1.7%.

1 Stakeholders

Everyone who is directly involved in a business has an interest in its future. Sometimes this is referred to as a vested interest, meaning that the people concerned stand to gain or lose financially. These interests embody a network of risks and rewards, as shown in Figure 4.1. Sometimes, the greater the risk, the greater the reward must be in order to induce people to take the risk.

The three main stakeholders within a company are the shareholders, the managers and the employees. The rewards for making their contribution to the business will vary. Some stakeholders take a lot of risk, whereas others do not. Although stakeholders' interests differ, they all want the business to succeed.

Figure 4.1 Risks and rewards

	When times are:		
Stakeholder	**Good**	**Bad**	**Very bad**
Shareholder	High dividend Capital gain	No dividend Capital loss	Lost capital
Manager	Lots of perks Bonus to salary	No perks Basic salary	Unemployed
Employee	Normal salary	Normal salary	Unemployed

There are areas of common interest, as shown in Figure 4.2, between the various stakeholders. This area of concern may not be as large as their individual interests, but it is there. In businesses where everyone is working together, this area of mutual concern is much larger.

Figure 4.2 The stakeholder model

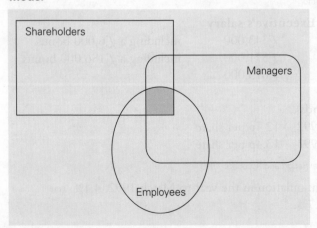

Parliament granted shareholders the right of limited liability in 1855 and since then the company, owned by shareholders, has become the most important form of business organisation. For many decades the shareholders were viewed as being the most important people associated with the business. This view has clearly changed and it is now recognised that many other groups of people are important to the company's success. The owners, in the form of shareholders, have a role in the company's future but so, too, do the employees and managers.

Traditionally, employees were not seen as having an interest in the long-term success of the company. Their interest was limited to getting paid at the end of the week and a good job was anything that paid well. This view has clearly changed and employees are now seen as having an important stake in the business, not least because they will lose their jobs if the company fails. Increasingly, companies are recognising that the workforce should be counted as part of the assets of the business, as it is their skills that create the profits. Sometimes this is reflected in the value of goodwill attached to a balance sheet at the time of a takeover.

Managers are interested in the performance of businesses, not just from an altruistic point of view, but because of the effects on their careers. Depending on the success of the business, managers can receive bonus payments, larger salaries, promotion, newer and larger cars, increased status, more staff etc. All these 'remunerations' recognise the managers' effectiveness and help their careers.

How much market power each of these groups has depends very much on the individual situation. To some degree, all three are protected by legislation and this greatly influences their respective positions both within the company and, collectively, as groups within society. Employee protection legislation gives individuals some safeguards against the demands of management. Trade union legislation protects management from the potential monopoly power of the trade unions. Legal requirements for the disclosure of information protect shareholders' rights and prevent managers from concealing things which shareholders might want to know. Market power is, in each case, subject to a range of checks and balances. The next three sections look at the position of each group in turn. The final section of this Enquiry shows how conflicts of interest may arise and how they may be handled.

2 Shareholders' powers

The modern company is owned by shareholders, be they individuals or corporations, and the company is supposed to pursue their interests. The company should respect the wishes of the shareholders, although it is often difficult to know exactly what the shareholders want. The shareholders' contribution to a company is often limited to their initial investment, from which they are entitled to the rewards of providing capital for a venture that has some risk associated with it. The extent of this risk varies between companies but, in all cases, the amount at risk is limited to the amount of money invested in the shares. This concept of **limited liability** is fundamental to the operation of companies.

As the owners of companies, shareholders receive dividends as the reward for their investment. They may also benefit from a rise in the value of their shares over a period of time. The dividend paid on different shares reflects the policies of each company as well as their success in the preceding year. To some extent, the share price of the company is an indication of how successful the stock market believes the company will be. If the company is thought to be doing well, then the expected dividends will be higher and therefore it is worth paying a larger amount for the share because the return, via the dividend, is greater.

Measuring share performance

Shareholders assess the performance of shares using (in addition to qualitative information) the price-earnings ratio and the yield. Their inclination to own the shares depends partly on such measures and if they are not satisfied with the performance of a share they own, they will probably sell it. Companies prefer to see their shares performing well and will try to keep their shareholders satisfied. In this way shareholder expectations do influence company behaviour.

Figure 4.3 shows shares which are quoted on the UK Stock Exchange with their yield and price earnings ratios.

Figure 4.3 Share prices

High	Low	Company	Price	Yield	Price/earning ratio
511	398	NatWest Bank	509	4.4%	30.5
584	426	Sainsbury	475	2.6%	16.7
563	454	Thames Water	501	5.2%	9.8

Source: *Financial Times*

Yield is measured as $\dfrac{\text{dividend per share}}{\text{market price of share}} \times 100$

This gives an indication of the current return on the existing value of the investment, assuming dividend payments remain constant.

The price/earnings ratio is measured by $\dfrac{\text{market price of the share}}{\text{earnings per share}}$

If a company has 5 million issued shares which are currently priced at 230p, the dividend payment is 15p per share, and net profit was £2 million, then earnings per share would be profit divided by the number of shares:

$\dfrac{£2m}{£5m}$ i.e. 40p. Then:

$$\text{Yield} = \frac{\text{dividend paid}}{\text{market price of share}} \times 100$$

$$= \frac{15 \times 100}{230}$$

$$= 6.52\%$$

$$\text{Price/earnings ratio} = \frac{\text{market price of the share}}{\text{earnings per share}}$$

$$= \frac{230p}{40p}$$

$$= 5.75$$

Associated Laundering plc

If you were considering buying shares in a public company, how would you rate Associated Laundering? The available information from the annual reports includes the following:

Turnover	£36m
Net profit	£1.2m
Dividend paid	20p
Issued shares	10million

From the newspaper you know the current price is 480p.

Shareholders' powers

The owners of ordinary shares have the right to vote at the company's annual general meetings. The shares can be resold on the stock exchange if they are shares in a public company. If they are shares in a private company, they can only be sold to family, friends and business associates. The **stock exchange** simply provides a market for second-hand shares; the buying and selling of shares on a daily basis does not provide additional capital.

Open Question

Should shareholders strive to influence company policy?

The theory of corporate ownership is that the company has numerous owners, who collectively appoint managers and directors to look after their investment. This traditional view of company ownership bears little resemblance to the reality of today's large organisations. The majority of the shares held in the companies quoted on the stock exchange are held by financial institutions such as pension funds and unit trusts. These businesses can have considerable influence over public companies because of their large share holdings. The threat of a large number of a company's shares being sold can give financial institutions a great deal of power. However, they may or may not be active in using it.

Aintree plc

Aintree is a medium-sized producer of sweets and assorted confectionery, based in Liverpool. In 1992 it was approached by a large national chocolate manufacturer which sought a takeover. The offer was very generous and valued the existing shares at a 25% premium over the current stock exchange value. Many small shareholders were very willing to sell and the chocolate manufacturer quickly gained 30% of all the shares. The directors of Aintree and the institutional shareholders thought the company was worth more and were not very keen to sell. To guarantee the loyalty of the institutional shareholders, the directors had to devise a plan for the reorganisation of the business as well as a rationalisation of the staff employed. This plan was developed in an attempt to boost profits and thereby increase the value of the company's shares, earning a greater return for the institutional shareholders.

Institutional versus individual shareholders

Traditionally, the only shareholders who have been able to exert any degree of power have been the large institutional owners. This position is beginning to change as shareholders recognise that they own companies and they all have a chance to influence the business, regardless of the size of their shareholding. By using the power of the media, even individual shareholders have been able to influence company behaviour.

Shareholders' power in the USA

Shareholders in the USA are becoming far more organised and many are attempting to reclaim the large companies as their own. Boards of directors are being lobbied with the demands of shareholders and the independent directors are being pressured to look after the shareholders, even if this is at the expense of the other board members. This movement has achieved some noticeable successes via the removal of prominent board members from Kodak, IBM and General Motors.

Figure 4.4 Share ownership

	% 1992
Insurance companies	16.5
Unit/investment trusts	6.2
Pension funds	34.7
Other financial institutions	3.4
Companies	1.8
Individuals	21.3
Public sector	1.5
Overseas	12.8
Other	1.8
	100%

Source: CSO, *Share Ownership Report*, end 1992

One of the objectives of the Conservative Government of 1979 was to encourage the widespread ownership of shares. In 1981 individuals owned only 28.2% of all the issued share capital in the UK. Figure 4.4 shows that that percentage has since fallen. However, the number of people owning shares within that total has grown because of the wider spread of share ownership achieved through privatisation. The dominance of institutional share ownership is clear.

Company insolvencies

There are risks for shareholders as well as rewards. Every year businesses fail, not always because they have made mistakes, and, consequently, the shareholders lose their investments in the shares.

Figure 4.5 Insolvencies

England and Wales

	1981	1982	1983	1984	1985	1986	1987	1988	1989	1990	1991
Companies	8,596	12,067	13,406	13,721	14,898	14,405	11,439	9,427	10,456	15,051	21,827
Individuals	5,151	5,700	7,032	8,229	6,778	7,155	7,427	8,507	9,365	13,987	25,640

Source: CSO, *Annual Abstract of Statistics*, 1993

Figure 4.5 shows the effects of the recession in the early 1990s. The advantages of forming a company, rather than trading as an individual or in a partnership, become very obvious during times of high bankruptcy rates.

The collapse of communism

The Central and Eastern European economies are heading for private ownership as quickly as possible. The move towards privatisation throughout Central Europe is creating new share-owning democracies in countries with very poorly developed financial markets. It is hard to understand the size of this transformation: for example the government of Czechoslovakia owned 96% of the country's output in 1986; in East Germany the figure was 97%.

The attempt to transfer some of these businesses to the private sector, via the issue of shares, has created many problems:

■ can foreigners buy shares?
■ what happens when there is no stock exchange?
■ will institutions be allowed to buy shares?
■ how do individuals sell shares?

It is easy to take share-owning democracies for granted and forget that the operation of a stock exchange requires a well-developed, sophisticated financial sector.

3 Employees' powers

Employees may be seen as a factor of production which employers will seek to obtain at the lowest possible cost. At the other extreme, they may be seen as the firm's greatest asset, to be nurtured and developed. Obviously, the former view leads to employees tending to have little or no power in the market. They are far more numerous than potential employers and may be in a 'take it or leave it' position in respect of their jobs.

This situation was very typical in the nineteenth century and led to the formation of trade unions. The only way in which employees could protect themselves from employer power was to join together to fight the often very harsh working conditions and poor wage rates.

Although working conditions have generally improved considerably, there are still some industries in which employee power may be very limited and there is a real need for representation by trade unions or professional associations. The establishment of UNISON in 1993 created the largest trade union in Europe. With 1.4 million members in the health and public service areas, it is able to provide a wide range of services beyond the traditional ones associated with a union. These include welfare support for those hit by misfortune, mortgage arrangements, insurance, legal advice and educational opportunities.

Trade unions can be in confrontational positions with employers. They can also have a very positive, collaborative role, working with management to enhance business performance and employee welfare. Much depends on the corporate culture of the business.

Trade union powers

**Supply of labour
Elasticity of supply**

A trade union can effectively create a monopoly. It can control the selling of labour to the employer, provided it can prevent non-members from being hired by the employer. If it can control the workforce, it can withdraw labour by strike action. This gives it considerable potential for the wielding of market power. It can limit the freedom of action of management quite effectively. Wages may be pushed above the competitive market rate. Figure 4.6 shows how, if the union can restrict the supply of labour and keep it rather inelastic, it may be able to raise wages.

Figure 4.6 Wage rates in the presence of a trade union

However, if a union does this, it may render the firm less competitive. By raising wages above what they would have been, it increases costs. This may mean that its efforts to protect its members backfire. The end result may be a loss of jobs as the employer seeks to regain competitiveness by reducing labour costs.

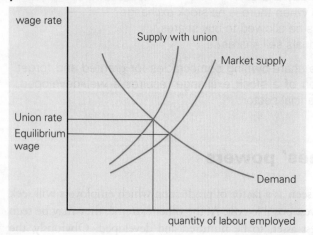

Restrictive practices

Although employees typically have little power as individuals, they may have much more if they act collectively. Sometimes employees can enhance their control over the workplace by the use of restrictive practices. Demarcation arrangements may prohibit anyone but the designated person from doing a certain job. This is supposed to protect jobs, but it also raises costs and reduces competitiveness. These restrictive practices are much less common than they used to be, although some still exist. For example, a nurse in the NHS may not change a plug on an electrical appliance; an electrician must be sent for, irrespective of whether the nurse can do the job properly.

Some unions have restricted entry to training programmes to those in the traditional age group for apprentices. This has hindered retraining programmes. Again, the objective was to preserve jobs.

Falling union membership

Although trade unions have seen their membership falling, they remain the largest voluntary organisations in the UK. In 1993 they still had 7.3 million members, who had all chosen to join.

Figure 4.7 Trade union membership and strikes

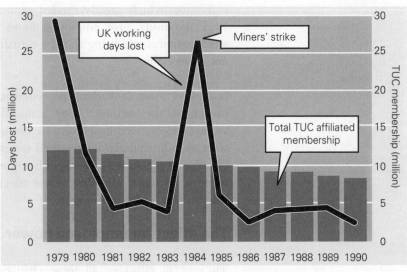

Source: Employment Gazette, 1991

Figure 4.7 shows how union membership fell during the 1980s, and the number of days lost in strike action. Many union members were employees in manufacturing industry. When large numbers of these were made redundant in the early 1980s recession, they dropped out of the union. As **Structural change** structural change led to increasingly capital-intensive production in manufacturing, this process of falling membership continued.

The other important factor in the loss of union membership was the way in which skilled people shifted towards dealing directly with their employers. Many such people are able to take care of themselves because the scarcity of their skills gives them quite considerable bargaining power even without the help of a union. They negotiate individual contracts with employers. They see little reason why they should join a union.

There are far fewer manual jobs than there used to be, so, as well as union membership falling, the relative size of different unions has changed. Unions representing manual workers have shrunk by more than average and the so-called 'white collar' unions have grown.

Legislative changes and union weakness

Generally speaking, the wage bargaining and restrictive practices described so far were intended to protect employees' pay, jobs and working conditions. However, in an open economy with strong competition from imports, they came to be seen as having the reverse effect. High costs and lack of competitiveness were seen by many people as destroying, not protecting, jobs. Increasingly poor industrial relations were one reason why voters elected the Conservative Government of 1979. As a result, during the 1980s there were changes in trade union legislation which greatly eroded union power. The intention was to weaken unions, give employers more freedom to introduce changed work practices and bring about a climate in which labour costs could be cut more easily.

Successive Acts of Parliament systematically weakened the bargaining power of the unions. They reduced the scope for picketing the workplace; allowed employers to sue unions for damages after certain sorts of industrial action; required secret ballots before a strike could be called; and prevented employees being required to join a union in order to do a particular job. Part of the effect on the unions is visible in the data on strike actions in Figure 4.7.

The effect on employee power

The overall effect of all these changes on the market power of the employee is not easy to determine. Through access to training and education, many people have seen their market power increase substantially because their scarce skills have been in demand. Many others, however, through vulnerability to unemployment, have found themselves with no power to improve their wages or working conditions whatsoever. The threat of unemployment has induced large numbers of people to accept new work practices. As a result, those who have remained in employment have benefited from increasing productivity and higher wages. Those who lost their jobs have seen a sharp reverse in their fortunes and, in some cases, have been forced to the margins of society.

Official picket line.

Overall, unions have become very much less powerful in the workplace as a result of the changes described.

Employees as assets

Human resource management

In recent years it has become clear that a business is more valuable if the employees are well motivated and successful. This view of employees as assets has spread from the service industries to manufacturing. The traditional view of 'us and them', encouraged by management in the past, is disappearing. Japanisation and the move to single-status employment patterns have done much to bring about the change.

Toyota

The new car factory in Derby opened for business in 1991 and with it came the Japanese attitude to employees. This was fundamentally different from the traditional pattern of employment in the British car industry. The difference in working habits soon became clear. No longer were staff controlled by foremen who were expected to regiment the shop-floor workers. The Japanese system relied on the employees managing their own time at work. This acts as a means of increasing motivation and hence company performance. Toyota has attempted to create 'a workplace where employees can take charge of their own destinies'.

Source: *The Economist*, 19 March 1994

A whole range of changes has meant that the position of the employee within the firm may now be very different from what it was traditionally. However, as much as conditions have improved for some, they have deteriorated for others. One firm may make strenuous efforts to take care of its employees. Another firm may be clinging to a precarious position and may react by taking people on temporarily, paying them poorly and giving little attention to the quality of their working conditions.

Recent research suggests that employee friendly work practices actually pay. Books written by Jeffrey Pfeffer (*Competitive Advantage Through People*, Harvard Business School Press, 1994) and Robert Waterman (*What America Does Right*, W.W. Norton, 1994) say that worker friendly employers are outperforming companies which claim profit as their prime objective. Self-managing teams, job security, training programmes for all and high wages are all strategies which can make the business more productive. However, they depend upon flexible management systems and these work well only when everyone is pulling their weight. They are, therefore, sometimes hard to put into effect.

A commitment to create employment conditions that suit people implies that employees have some control over their working situation. Power is perhaps an inappropriate word for the gains involved. Nevertheless, the trend towards a collaborative attitude on the part of employers implies a sharing of power.

Family friendly employers

THE Alliance and Leicester Building Society has adopted family friendly policies. It argues that its term-time working arrangements for parents, the option of 10 weeks' unpaid leave with employment rights protected and flexi-time, make good business sense, attracting and retaining quality staff.

In retailing, Boots introduced family-friendly policies to reduce turnover of its 35,000 staff by 1% and therefore employees' costs per head. Its policies include part-time working, job sharing, flexi-time, maternity and paternity leave, a summer activity scheme for children and a nursery play scheme. Despite the recession, Boots has taken a long-term strategic view of its staffing levels and benefits, while other companies have preferred short-term options, such as reducing staff numbers or, for example, relaxing child-care provision.

The company now has 50% of women on maternity leave returning, compared with 7% four years ago.

Boots does not just calculate policy benefits in financial terms – it believes staff commitment and loyalty are as valuable, if more difficult to quantify.

Source: *Financial Times*, 11 April 1994

The legal framework

The relationship between the employers and the employees within any organisation is controlled mainly by their contract of employment. This contract has to conform to the current statutory requirements. Most of the behaviour of people at work occurs without reference to their contracts but if things start to go wrong, then the contract becomes important.

In UK law there is a basic distinction between those who are self-employed and those who are employed. In the former case, the contract will be very different and the amount of statutory protection will be more limited. Employed people are entitled to receive a contract of employment within 13 weeks of starting work. This contract should include the date work started; the scale of pay; when wages are paid; hours of work; holiday, sick pay and pension details; length of notice to be given; disciplinary rules and grievance procedures.

There are three types of employment contract – permanent, temporary and personal. Each type of contract gives the worker certain rights and responsibilities, although the rights afforded to employees on temporary contracts are few because employers can include 'waiver clauses'. These clauses often deny the worker the right to claim redundancy pay or unfair dismissal if the contract is not renewed.

New-style contracts

Many organisations are introducing contracts based on a minimum number of guaranteed hours of employment. This could be 20 or it could be zero hours. The idea is that the company can then ask its workers, often at very short notice, to work longer hours when there is work to do. In retailing, an eight-hour contract is appearing, whereby employees are given work during the busy times in the week but may not be employed during weekdays when trade is slack. The difference between this and a Saturday job is that employees sign contracts to say they are available and prepared to work longer hours if called upon by the company. This increased flexibility is very beneficial to the company.

These three types of employment contract create more flexibility for an employer and allow businesses to respond to changes in their markets. This move in the 1980s, towards deregulating the labour market and the introduction of more flexible contracts of employment, has reduced the protection granted to workers. The growth of temporary, casual and part-time employees within the workforce has given Britain the highest number of part-time employees of any European Union state.

Open Question

Has the employee's position improved or deteriorated during the 1980s and 1990s?

All employees working more than 16 hours per week have the right to redundancy pay, maternity leave and unfair dismissal protection after two years of continuous employment. Employees working between eight and 16 hours per week must wait five years for these rights.

Redundancy

This is defined by the Employment Protection Act 1978 as those dismissals attributable to one or more of the following reasons:

1 The employer has ceased to carry on business.
2 The employer has ceased to carry on business in the place where the employee was employed.
3 The employer's need for employees to carry on work of a particular kind has ceased or diminished.

In these cases of unemployment, the employee is entitled to a redundancy payment.

Dismissal

If an employee is dismissed from a job it may be that the law regards this as unfair. Clearly, not all dismissals are unfair, but sometimes the employer abuses the power available at the expense of employees. The law recognises that employees are entitled to some protection through the Employment Protection Acts of 1978 and 1980. There are some fair reasons for dismissal, however, and an employee claiming unfair dismissal might have to convince a tribunal that the dismissal was unfair.

Equal opportunities legislation

Throughout the European Union there are regulations about the treatment of employees. UK legislation requires equal treatment of workers and ensures that there is no discrimination on the grounds of race or gender. However, it remains the case that, on average, women are paid less than men, even when doing a similar job. Their bargaining power in the labour market is usually less.

Market imperfections

Any kind of discrimination indicates a market imperfection. It implies that able-bodied white men face less competition than they would in a discrimination-free labour market. Their earnings will be higher than they need be, just as those of other groups will be lower than they could be.

Open Question

Can discrimination reduce efficiency?

The 1970 **Equal Pay Act** was introduced to end discrimination between men and women. It was amended in 1984 to enable men and women to claim equal wages for work of equal value done for the same employer or an associated employer.

In 1991 a case taken forward by the trade union GMB and the Equal Opportunities Commission established that the work done by storemen was of equal value to work done by three women working as office clerks. After a seven-year battle, the office clerks were awarded £15,000 compensation and a £40 a week pay rise.

The **Sex Discrimination Acts of 1975 and 1986** declare that it is unlawful to be less favourably treated because of your sex or because you are married.

Dismissal because of pregnancy

A recent European Court ruling has extended the rights of working women who become pregnant. The claimant had worked for a UK building society for just over a year when she became pregnant. She was unable to claim protection from dismissal as she had not worked for the qualifying two-year period but when her boss said she would not be able to return to employment after the birth, she took legal advice. The European Court ruled that to lose a job for being pregnant is to lose a job because you are a woman and is clearly sex discrimination. Because of the European Court ruling, the claimant was able to take maternity leave and return to her job after the birth.

The **Race Relations Act 1976** outlaws all racial discrimination. It also established the Commission for Racial Equality which has direct responsibility for monitoring the effect of the Act. Despite the existence of the law, it is clear that discrimination still occurs: being a member of a racial minority reduces market power. The outcome is visible not so much in terms of lower pay, as is the case with women, as in higher unemployment.

Black joblessness blamed on race bias

DISCRIMINATION is the main reason why black people in Britain face an unemployment rate three times as high as that facing whites, according to a Trade Union Congress report on black workers in the labour market published today.

'What recovery there has been in the labour market has completely bypassed the black workforce,' said Mr John Monks, general secretary, yesterday. 'Evidence suggests they are the last to be hired and the first to be fired.'

The study suggests the sort of jobs black workers do does not provide an explanation for the higher unemployment rate.

It says black workers are mainly under-represented in recession-prone industries such as construction. The report says: 'The geographical concentration of ethnic minority workers can only explain some of the differences. Nor can lack of qualifications be a convincing explanation.'

Source: *Financial Times*, 15 April 1994

The costs of employee protection

Some employers express concern because equal opportunities and some contractual obligations raise the cost of employing labour. If they do, they may lead to fewer jobs being created. There is a clear conflict of interest between the need for a flexible labour force, which can meet employers' needs at low cost, and the protection of employees' rights. Other employers would claim that treating employees properly will help to motivate them and increase productivity.

4 Managers' interests

Figure 4.8 The managerial process

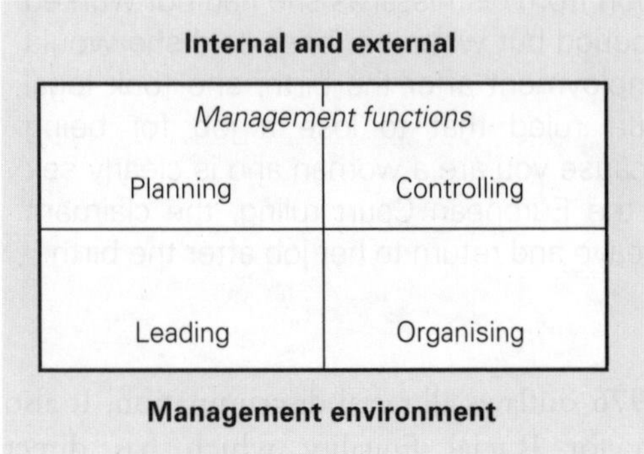

Internal and external

Management functions	
Planning	Controlling
Leading	Organising

Management environment

The managerial process consists of four basic functions: **planning, controlling, leading** and **organising**. Figure 4.8 shows these functions, which were identified by Henri Fayol. They provide the means by which managers try to achieve the objectives of the business. The manager's power to operate without restrictions is limited by the changing internal environment of the business as well as the external environment within the market and the overall economy.

Planning – involves the setting of objectives and the development of action plans to meet these objectives. This process focuses attention on objectives, anticipating problems and eradicating uncertainties.

Organising – involves acquiring resources (both human and physical) and working towards objectives. There are various ways of organising staff and the approach taken will depend on the company's history as well as the management style. Staff may be organised in hierarchical or team based systems, in functional and task-based groups.

Leading – involves motivating people and controlling the rewards paid. Individuals who are not highly inspirational can still learn to be effective leaders. There are different types of leaders within any organisation. A leadership grid can be used to identify leaders according to their concern for people and their concern for the company's products. The five types of leader categorised are shown in Figure 4.9.

A – concentrates on looking after the people within the organisation with little regard for the product. Often known as country club management.

B – emphasises both people and the product. Often known as team management.

C – middle-of-the-road management style.

Figure 4.9 The leadership grid

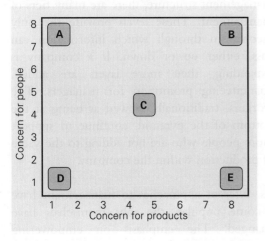

D – impoverished style and little if any leadership shown.
E – authoritative style with little regard for people.

Controlling is the ability to make a comparison between planned events and actual events so as to monitor performance continuously. All managers must be able to identify problems and sort out why things are going wrong.

To the extent that managers actually do plan, organise, lead and control, they may have considerable power within the business. Exercising that power effectively will depend on the extent to which they have developed managerial skills. Whether managers have power *beyond* the business itself depends upon many other factors. The business environment may constrain them very greatly.

Entrepreneurial skills are just one aspect of managerial capability; there are many others. Technical skills involve knowledge of machinery and processes. Interpersonal skills involve the ability to lead and motivate, to communicate effectively, to listen and demonstrate empathy. Conceptual skills are involved in understanding and co-ordinating the full range of activities within the organisation. The possession of a wide range of skills can enable managers to use their powers effectively.

The changing nature of management

Delayering

Delayering has resulted in there being fewer managers and in those who remain having a much greater span of control. This change in structure has had an enormous effect on the management of organisations.

In this changed style of organisation, it can be more difficult to motivate managers. The traditional rewards associated with successful management may no longer be available. Delayering reduces the opportunities for promotion. Managers clearly have a stake in the success of a business and they deserve to be rewarded when things go well because they will certainly lose out when things go badly. In many ways, they share the risks associated with being in business, although not to the extent that shareholders are exposed to risk. The changing nature of hierarchies has been accompanied by three developments in management:

1 The use of more sophisticated appraisal systems which include the setting of objectives and the identification of training needs.
2 The move towards more systematic procedures, particularly in areas of recruitment, performance assessment and training.
3 Linkage between pay and individual performance, usually based on a market comparison.

'It's our parent company. We're not to drink too much and we must be home early.'

Source: Williams in *Squib*,
Oct.– Nov. 1993

In the extreme case of a hierarchical management structure, there are many tiers of management. These levels provide the only mechanism through which information can pass, either up or down. If a company is expanding, then more layers are added, guaranteeing promotion for managers. The workers, traditionally viewed as being at the bottom of the pyramid, continue to support more people who are not adding to the value of production within the company.

As different approaches to management have become popular, the jobs themselves have changed. The emphasis on empowering managers so that they do not need supervision and monitoring is an attempt to reduce the bureaucratic nature of organisations. During and since the 1980s, companies have found that delayering can have beneficial effects in terms of profits as well as improved communications from top to bottom. There are considerable cost savings and for those managers who have remained, their jobs have changed significantly. They have had to become more generalist, with greater responsibilities and a wider range of tasks. In addition, managers are likely to find themselves with an increasingly diverse mixture of staff within their span of control, creating potential problems of motivation. This suggests that managerial power is increasing. Managers are being encouraged to have more autonomy and control a wider area of work.

So what power do managers actually have?

In some ways, the ability to hire and fire staff has increased because of the changes in government legislation and the reduction in the strength of the trade union movement. Many managers are expected to take on more responsibilities and to have more skills than before. They are also expected to be more accountable for their own performance. If things are not going well, the blame cannot so easily be passed on to the workforce. Managers, like all of the staff, are employees and have to take their instructions from the senior managers and directors. They are just as likely to lose their jobs for a poor performance as are the staff. However, they do, to a degree, have the power to motivate their staff and to decide some of the company's tactics.

Should managers always follow the instructions they are given by the board of directors? Should managers accept contracts to sell products to countries where the leaders do not respect human rights? How should managers respond to their company becoming involved in activities that offend a manager's conscience? Is there a divide between what someone does at work and what they do at home? These are difficult questions which some managers may have to face. In difficult situations they may feel powerless because they have less room for manoeuvre than they would like.

5 Conflicts and collaboration

Golden handshakes

When company profits start to fall, it isn't just the employees who suffer through redundancy. Shareholders expect the leaders of the company to re-examine their own positions and in some cases in the 1980s and 1990s Chief Executives and directors have left. When this happens these executives often receive very large pay-offs to compensate for the loss of office. Sir Ralph Halpern left Burtons in 1990 with a lump sum of £1.6 million and a pension of £456,000 per year for life. Gerald Ratner left Ratners in 1992 with a year's salary of £375,000. Sir Nigel Broackes and Sir Eric Parker, who built up the Trafalgar House conglomerate in the 70s and 80s, left with £750,000 and £1.3 million respectively in 1993.

These payouts contrast with the redundancy deals offered to the workers within these organisations.

The legal requirement for redundancy in the UK depends on the length of employment and your age. The maximum payment available is currently £6,150 for a 64-year-old with 20 years' service.

Conflicts of interest arise when decisions made in the interests of one group of stakeholders are found to be against the interests of another group of stakeholders. A conflict of interest will usually mean that there is an ethical question: *ought* one party to gain at the expense of another?

Many companies have justified their particular actions by reference to the interests of their shareholders, who expect profits to be made in order to fund dividends. While this may have been an acceptable answer one hundred years ago, there is now increasing recognition that companies have much wider responsibilities. Successful businesses have to be able to satisfy all their stakeholders, from customer to society, as well as the shareholder. They are expected to achieve a whole range of objectives, taking in the interests of all their stakeholders. Some companies have recognised that they have to be responsible for their actions. Marks and Spencer has always had a policy of looking after its employees and customers. In this way, it expects to secure greater profits and a higher share price than other retailers, thereby satisfying its owners too. But not all firms see things this way. Conflicts of interest are thus inevitable.

Employee involvement (EI)

Involving the workforce in the business is one way of motivating people. This does not mean that management must give up power and authority, but they should try to get the best from employees. A scheme to involve employees could consist of team briefings (downward communication); quality circles (upward communication); and joint consultation (representative participation).

Managers are interested in involving workers *not* as a means of control but as a way of gaining the workforce's commitment and informing and educating all employees. Involvement may produce ideas, defuse tensions at work and help to attract quality staff.

Figure 4.10 Employee involvement

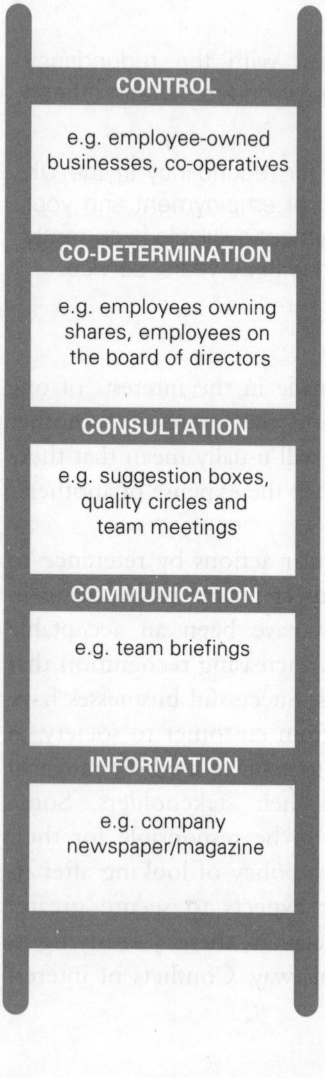

There are different levels of employee involvement. Some are formally recognised while others, particularly in small businesses, are very informal. The extent of involvement can be considered as a set of steps, with differing degrees of influence on final decisions. These are shown as a ladder in Figure 4.10.

Some managers resist the idea of employee involvement. Others introduce it to some degree but treat it as a cosmetic exercise. Managerial opposition is one factor in the UK government's opposition to the social chapter of the Maastricht agreement. There is no objective evidence of it harming company performance; rather the reverse. It appears that some managers perceive employee involvement as creating a conflict of interest, while others would deny that this exists.

CONTROL

e.g. employee-owned businesses, co-operatives

CO-DETERMINATION

e.g. employees owning shares, employees on the board of directors

CONSULTATION

e.g. suggestion boxes, quality circles and team meetings

COMMUNICATION

e.g. team briefings

INFORMATION

e.g. company newspaper/magazine

Share incentive schemes

MR Paddy Ashdown, Liberal Democrat leader, yesterday called for a big increase in the use of share incentive schemes to improve industrial competitiveness.

He said that wider employee share ownership was part of the answer to the 'fundamental question' of how to compete with Pacific-rim economies without endangering social cohesion. He said that only 55% of British companies used bonus schemes, and only a sixth of companies with share incentive schemes had extended them to non-executive staff.

Mr Ashdown told the Involvement and Participation Association, a business group, that tax incentives should be used to increase employee shareholdings. He pledged that a Liberal Democrat government would give employees the right to participate in decision making if companies failed to set up voluntary consultation.

He said: 'My message to industry is this. If you don't want compulsory structures for consulting employees, prove that you are ... practising genuine employee involvement.'

Source: *Financial Times*, 17 March 1994

Flexible labour markets versus employee protection

The UK has a flexible labour market compared to other EU countries, although it is rather less flexible than that of the USA. In this context, flexibility means that employers find it easy both to hire and fire and, in general, that the workforce is responsive to employers' needs. Flexible labour markets have relatively little government regulation of employment practices. The employer's market power is enhanced at the expense of that of the employee.

Employing people on short-term contracts and using part-time employees both make for flexibility. Regulations concerning redundancy and contractual obligations create market imperfections and make for less flexibility. The worry is that if employers find it hard to get rid of people once they are on the payroll, they may think twice about hiring them at all, so fewer jobs may be created.

The evidence for this can be seen in the data for Europe as a whole and the USA. Figure 4.11 shows the percentage of labour in employment in both. Whereas both started out with about 65% in employment in 1973, by the early 1990s the USA had about 72% in employment, against 62% in Europe. (Using employment data gets away from the problems caused by the use of different measures of unemployment.) More of the jobs created in the USA have been full time. Furthermore, people who lose their jobs in the USA tend to find another faster than would be the case in Europe. However, labour turnover is higher in the USA – 2% of USA employees become unemployed each month, against 0.4% in Europe.

The drawback to the US approach is that it entails more inequality. Figure 4.12 shows how much worse off the poorest American workers are than the average. Further, unemployment benefits are very low and do not last long.

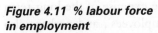

Figure 4.11 % labour force in employment

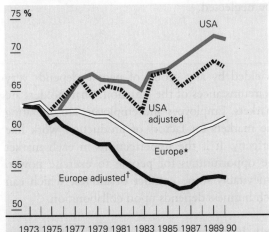

1973 1975 1977 1979 1981 1983 1985 1987 1989 90

*Austria, Belgium, Britain, Denmark, France, Finland, Germany, Greece, The Netherlands, Iceland, Ireland, Italy, Norway, Portugal, Spain, Sweden, Switzerland, Turkey
†Finland, France, Germany, The Netherlands, Italy, Norway, Spain, Sweden

Source: OECD

Figure 4.12 Median, high and low pay in the USA, compared to pay in Europe

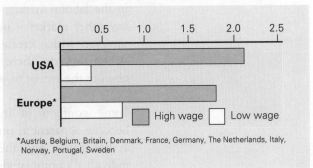

*Austria, Belgium, Britain, Denmark, France, Germany, The Netherlands, Italy, Norway, Portugal, Sweden

Source: OECD

Is it better to have lower unemployment or better job protection for those in work?

The US labour market ensures that more jobs are available and contributes to the general prosperity of the nation. The price of this is a problem of poverty for some people, which is worse than that of Europe, and a high degree of job insecurity. The UK can choose between protecting jobs more as in the rest of the EU, or increasing flexibility and moving towards the US approach.

Short termism

Quite often, it is said that UK business is guilty of going for quick profits rather than investing in the future. It is true that many businesses have used investment criteria (such as the payback period) which emphasise the speed with which returns can be obtained. Further, the threat of takeover has often meant that companies have been under pressure to provide large dividends in an attempt to keep shareholders loyal. This means that less profit is retained and ploughed back in the form of capital investment which would provide future growth.

Research has compared the UK with the German experience. Germany is generally thought to be less prone to short termism. German firms do pay out lower dividends than large UK firms; they are less likely to be threatened with takeover as there is less takeover activity there. Small firms in Germany find it easier to obtain bank finance than their counterparts in the UK. This reduces reliance on equity finance.

If shareholders' interests are attended to at the expense of the long-term growth and health of the company, then employees', and perhaps also managers', interests may be neglected.

Conclusions

The amount of power wielded by any group of people depends very heavily on the individual circumstances of the situation. Shareholders are operating in the capital markets. Employees and employers are operating in the labour market. The markets for factors of production work like any other market – imperfectly. It is the imperfections in each market situation which create the opportunities for people to exercise power. When they do, there is inevitably some conflict of interest which can obscure the extent to which business depends upon collaboration.

Some conflicts of interest have been described here. Others may become apparent as time goes by. In business, whether interests are seen as being one and the same or as conflicting often depends on the individual's point of view. Wherever a conflict exists there will be scope for government involvement. It is to this that the next Enquiry turns.

Enquiry 5: What powers are applied by the government?

Scope

Governments everywhere need to determine a framework of rules for business activity. A modern economy is based on a vast network of rules which form a common framework for all business decisions. This framework helps to reduce uncertainty, by requiring people to abide by the terms of the contracts they enter into, and by ensuring that relevant information is available. However, government control goes even further, by regulating activity 'in the public interest'. Here the objective is to create 'a level playing-field' so that firms compete on roughly equal terms, and to protect consumers from producer power. However, although these are the overall objectives, there are many inconsistencies in the approach to them.

Enquiry 4 looked at the role of the government in the labour market. This Enquiry concentrates on the role of the government in controlling business more generally.

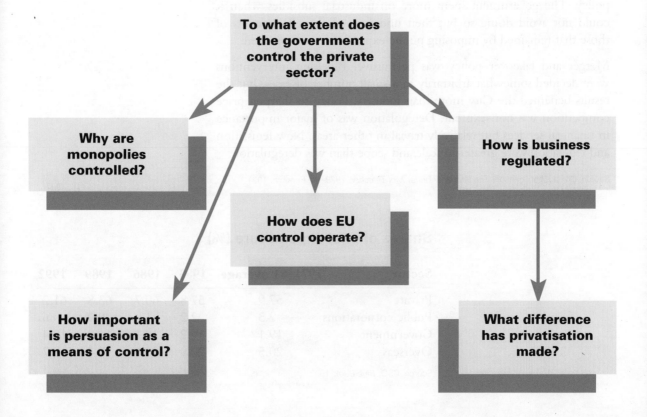

Opening evidence

The Department of Trade and Industry view

UNDER EU law, anti-competitive practices are prohibited. Companies which collaborate to fix prices or try to force competitors out of the market can be fined up to 10% of their world-wide turnover. In the UK, businesses accused of anti-competitive behaviour are first investigated by the competition authorities. If the accusation is upheld, they will be required to give an undertaking that they will not repeat the anti-competitive behaviour. So the deterrents to such behaviour are much weaker under UK law than under EU law.

In the UK, a business is considered to have a scale monopoly if it has 25% of the market, irrespective of whether it has real market power. But because of the case-by-case approach described above, it may be decided that although a monopoly exists, the business is not actually abusing its power. The system is flexible.

Under EU rules, actual dominance is the issue. The European Commission takes the view that a dominant position exists when a business has at least 40% of the market and its rivals have significantly smaller shares. Other factors, such as barriers to entry for new competitors and anti-competitive behaviour are also relevant.

Source: *Financial Times*, 1 December 1992

An assessment of industrial policy in the 1980s

The frequent changes of ministers in charge of trade and industry was disruptive and coincided with bewildering shifts in the content of policy. The government spent more on industrial subsidies when it could not avoid doing so but then undermined the effectiveness of those that remained by imposing public expenditure cuts on them.

Merger and takeover policy was permissive. Blocking interventions were decided somewhat arbitrarily in a small number of cases, but the results benefited the City more than industry. Policy to sharpen price competition was non-existent. Deregulation was of major importance in financial services but relatively trivial in other areas. New legislation and regulation were greater in scale and scope than was deregulation.

Source: Christopher Johnson, *The Economy Under Mrs Thatcher, 1979–90*, Penguin, 1991

Shares of final expenditure (%)

Sector	1971–81 average	1983	1986	1989	1992
Private	57.9	57.8	60.7	63.8	61.2
Public corporations	2.5	2.2	1.0	0.9	0.6
Government	19.1	19.2	18.1	16.9	19.4
Overseas	20.5	20.9	20.1	18.4	18.7

Source: CSO, *Blue Book*, 1993

Gross Domestic Product

Year	GDP (current prices) £	Government expenditure £	As (%) of GDP
1982	279,041	128,755	46.1
1983	304,456	138,521	45.5
1984	325,852	147,218	45.2
1985	357,344	157,764	44.1
1986	384,843	162,331	38.3
1987	423,381	169,222	40.0
1988	471,430	178,213	37.8
1989	515,957	197,026	38.2
1990	551,118	215,556	39.1
1991	573,645	228,342	39.8
1992	596,165	254,126	42.6

Source: CSO, *Blue Book*, 1993

Compulsory competitive tendering

Since 1979 the Government has aimed at reducing the number of public sector workers, reducing the public sector pay bill and increasing the share of the economy in which market forces can operate.

Source: HM Treasury, *Using Private Enterprise in Government*, 1986

One of the ways in which the private sector has been more actively involved in public sector services has been through the compulsory competitive tendering process, introduced through legislation in 1980 and 1988. The legislation requires major council services, such as refuse collection, street cleaning, vehicle maintenance, etc. to be put out for tender. The local councils can bid for the work. If they are unsuccessful the directly employed workers will lose their jobs, but they can be taken on by the successful bidders. Since July 1993, following a European Court ruling, any workers that are re-employed by the successful bidder must stay on the same pay and conditions.

Since 1988 nearly 65% of Civil Service jobs (approximately 350,000) have been moved into newly formed executive agencies, which are responsible for running government services. The target figure of 75% of all Civil Service jobs to be open to compulsory competitive tendering will create more opportunities for private sector organisations to bid for the work.

The EU view

The European Union's view on competition is very clear. In an OECD publication in 1984 it declared: 'Competition has as its central economic goal the preservation and promotion of the competitive process, a process which encourages efficiency in the production and allocation of goods and services, and over time, through its effects on innovation and adjustment to technological change, a dynamic process of sustained economic growth. In conditions of effective competition, rivals have equal opportunity to compete for business on the basis and quality of their outputs, and resource deployment follows market success in meeting consumers' demand at the lowest possible cost.'

1 The government and the market

Markets are a kind of contest between sellers and buyers. The government has always had the task of being referee through setting rules for fair trade and ensuring their proper enforcement. Today that role is much enlarged and the government also exercises a substantial degree of market power in its own right.

The 'referee' function has become extensive and complex. The government's powers expanded quickly during the nineteenth century. A legal framework for corporate enterprise, the treatment of employees and the protection of consumers were all areas of increasing intervention. Until the Second World War, however, governments remained on the 'touchline' of the economy, believing that market forces should take their own course. This view was radically changed by the Great Depression of the 1930s and the experience of directing the economy towards military victory in war. After 1945 the government established and funded the welfare state. It nationalised a range of key industries that were to be run 'in the public interest'. Finally, it accepted responsibility for steering the economy towards the macroeconomic objectives of full employment, economic growth, stable prices and balanced trade.

Within the economy, the government thus became both a referee and a player. Protection for consumers and employees was extended. Market imperfections were finally addressed with legislation to control monopoly (1948), restrictive trade practices (1956) and mergers (1965). The public sector quickly became a huge economic estate in its own right. Through ministerial departments, the nationalised industries and local councils, the government gained serious market power, both as a buyer and as a seller. At the same time, the much higher levels of taxation and spending became important influences on the level of aggregate demand and on the distribution of income.

Fiscal policy

Fine tuning the economy and controlling markets became the normal business of governments. However, the emphasis of government policy has changed significantly since 1979. Where possible, the government has withdrawn from direct provision and intervention in the market. The programme for privatisation and deregulation has combined a major government retreat from direct provision of goods and services with a more exacting supervision of the new markets in which private enterprise is free to operate. The emphasis has moved away from manipulating demand or originating supply. Instead, the aim is to create the supply-side conditions within which the normal producer-consumer relations of the market may function most effectively. The government remains a real source of power in many markets. There has been no simple return to the era of *laissez-faire* but competitive private enterprise has become the preferred agent of economic activity while the government increasingly concentrates on the roles of facilitator, regulator and referee.

Privatisation

Privatisation, the sale of a state-owned business to the private sector, means that the new owners will be both individual shareholders and institutions. It has been a major development throughout the western world over the past 15 years. Even in countries like France, where the government has traditionally owned and controlled large sections of industry and commerce, the trend is unmistakable. France began its first privatisation programme in September 1993 with the sale of government-owned shares in banks, a car company, an airline, shipping firms and many others.

British Airports Authority

One of the earliest state-owned businesses to be sold into the private sector was the British Airports Authority, now BAA. This is the organisation which owns the major UK airports such as Gatwick, Heathrow and Glasgow. It had always been a very profitable business and remains so. It has two main sources of income:

■ charges to the airlines to land their planes
■ charges to various users to put their businesses on BAA's land.

Users of the land include car parking companies, storage companies, duty-free shops, etc.

The theory is that commercial pressures force decision takers in the private sector to be more efficient than they would be if backed by the government.

For privatisation to be a success in terms of increasing competition and thereby benefiting the consumer, the OECD suggests that there are four principles to follow:

1 The industry should be restructured before it is privatised to ensure there is competition.
2 When some of the activities of the new organisation are in monopolistic markets, these activities should form a separate organisation. This will ensure that excessive profits from a monopoly cannot be used to subsidise a less efficient activity which is facing stronger competition.
3 New businesses should be subject to all the usual legislation that prevents anti-competitive behaviour.
4 Extra pro-competition legislation may be necessary, after privatisation, to prevent the new business from taking advantage of its position.

However, the UK government has not always adhered to these principles. Some attempts have been made to break up some industries. For example, the electricity industry was split into two generators, National Power and Powergen, and 12 regional distribution companies. This is supposed to promote competition, although, in reality, it may do so only to a limited degree. Other industries were left as clear-cut monopolies: water is a case in point. Despite the fact that the government allowed some competition in telecommunications from Mercury and others, BT continues to have considerable market power.

A major factor in the government's decisions about privatisation was its fear that if the privatised industries faced too much competition, shares in them would not be attractive to potential investors. The greater the competition, the harder the company must work to make a profit. The less the competition, the higher the dividends were likely to be. So the government left open the possibility of monopoly profits in some industries in order to ensure that the sales were successful. There was also a persistent tendency for shares to be underpriced when offered to the market, again in order to be sure that they sold.

Water privatisation

Many people were doubtful about the wisdom of privatising water. The supply of water is a natural monopoly and competition is difficult to arrange. It seemed that there would be scope for large price increases. In addition, there was clearly a need to bring water supplies up to EU standards.

Before privatisation the water companies could spend only a limited amount on cleaning up rivers and water supplies. Once in the hands of individual and institutional shareholders, the companies could decide freely how much to spend on the clean-up. They began a massive investment in new technologies and measures to reduce pollution. Water charges rose much faster than the rate of inflation. The ten water companies' profits rose impressively.

Do the high profits mean that efficiency has increased? Or do they mean that prices were raised more than they need have been to pay for the environmental improvements? If the latter is true, is tighter regulation called for?

Open Question

Has privatisation been of benefit to the consumer?

The profits made by the privatised industries have, in general, been high. The result has been growing pressure to tighten regulatory systems and prevent them from exploiting their monopoly power.

2 Regulation and deregulation

OFWAT

THE Office of Water Services (OFWAT), set up in 1989, is an independent government body responsible for ensuring that the water and sewerage companies provide a good quality and efficient service at a fair price. OFWAT sets an upper limit to the price increases allowed each year. It is also charged with finding ways to increase the scope for competition in the water industry. As a result, large users are allowed to 'shop around' for the cheapest supply.

The water companies find OFWAT's requirements rather tough to deal with. They have complained bitterly about them. Their comments prompted the following response in a *Financial Times* leader column. It addresses the issues of regulation generally, although water was in the news at the time.

'While shareholders and consumers have both done well out of the utilities since privatisation, it is the shareholders who have had the better deal. The government was insufficiently ambitious, early on, in introducing competition into hitherto monopolistic industries; pricing formulas did not take into account the full scope for efficiency gains. Now that the pricing arrangements have been tightened and increased competition brought to bear, both management and investors feel uncomfortable. That is precisely what ought to be happening. There is no reason why customers should, in the words of Mr Ian Byatt of OFWAT, find themselves on "an endless price escalator". Nor should utilities be an engine of inflation in the wider economy.'

Source: *Financial Times*, 15 April 1994

All the natural monopolies which were privatised were given a watchdog body to regulate them. This was considered essential to protect the consumer. The pattern which developed was for the watchdog to specify a maximum price rise allowable, over and above the rate of inflation. Water, which faced the requirement for major and expensive investment in improving quality, was allowed to raise prices by more than inflation. BT, which was expected to make big cost savings as a result of improved technologies, was allowed price increases well below inflation.

It would appear that the regulators are badly needed if utilities with monopoly powers are not to be allowed to raise prices excessively. But the regulators consist of small organisations with limited resources. They may not always be able to resist the complaints of the companies. They need support from the government if they are to do the job properly. There is still scope for water companies to make efficiency improvements similar to those that have been made in other privatised industries.

Deregulation

The idea behind deregulation is to 'roll back' the frontiers of the state and allow the private sector to manage and control its own affairs. This reflects the view that markets will be more competitive if businesses are left to make decisions without interference. Some of the main examples of deregulation have been within the financial markets; during the 1990s the impetus for deregulation has increased in other areas.

The deregulation of the banks proved to be a mixed blessing. Starting in 1981, the Bank of England encouraged the banks to compete much more energetically for business. This was expected to make the banks more efficient and encourage them to offer a better service. In this it was successful to a degree but one of the consequences was that each bank had an incentive to increase its lending as much as it could.

As the 1980s wore on and the economy boomed, banks lent to more and more businesses. They also financed a huge increase in consumer spending, which contributed to the overheating of the economy. Inflation began to accelerate and by 1988 the government felt bound to change to a counter-inflation policy and high interest rates. Many borrowers were hit very hard by the interest charges and had to cut back spending considerably. The story ends with the economy in a very severe recession. At the very least, the consequences of bank deregulation should have been recognised sooner. The deregulation of financial markets is not confined to the UK. Other countries also followed the familiar cycle of boom followed by recession.

In 1989 the 24 member countries of the OECD agreed to amend their codes of behaviour to allow greater capital movements and associated trade in banking and financial services. It seems likely that this could benefit the UK financial services sector as its export revenue may increase.

The reasons for deregulation

The main reason cited for the removal of state controls over business is the increase in efficiency that arises from more competition. The existence of controls, procedures and regulations is thought to restrict business activity. They prevent companies from taking advantage of market opportunities and impede their ability to respond to new circumstances. Some politicians have argued that regulations prevent the business community from managing its own affairs and create unnecessary hurdles not always faced by our overseas competitors. To the extent that deregulation increases efficiency, it should be of benefit to both consumers and producers. By giving businesses more opportunity to control their own destinies, deregulation will encourage the economy to expand. The snag is that deregulation has, in so many cases, brought with it unexpected consequences which have been much less beneficial.

The pensions industry

Traditionally, most employees were faced with two types of pension: one provided by the state and one provided by their company. Not everyone had a company pension scheme; they would have to rely on the government-provided state pension. For people who had a company scheme and changed jobs during their career, it was very difficult to build up a large pension with one company as few employers would allow a worker to transfer into their scheme with their existing pension credits.

The government changed this system in July 1988 and introduced the idea of a personal pension. Now an employee can take out his or her own pension with any provider, be it a bank, a building society, or insurance company. Employees are not tied to the company for which they work; they take their pensions with them wherever they are employed. The individual can control the size of the pension at the time of retirement by contributing more or less. The pension providers invest these contributions and make a profit from this business. The changes seemed likely to make it easier for people to change jobs and therefore looked like a sensible measure to increase flexibility.

However, there was a snag. People who sell pension plans are required to be very accurate in the advice they give to potential customers. Unfortunately, many of the people selling personal pensions failed to alert their clients to the fact that what they were selling offered a rather worse return than the typical occupational pension. The situation was so serious that a compensation scheme had to be devised. Effectively, some members of the public had been defrauded.

What had happened was that the old system had been deregulated but the controls put in place to ensure that inaccurate or incomplete financial advice was not given, proved inadequate.

Deregulation can involve a loss of jobs. A decline in safety standards may occur and businesses may take advantage of their monopoly power. What actually happens depends on the situation in the industry concerned. Deregulating bus services may have led to improved provision but it is not yet clear whether this will be maintained.

Open Question

Can deregulation benefit the consumer?

In some markets there seem to be very few advantages in deregulating control over standards. For example, it would appear unwise to reduce controls over the introduction of new medicines on to the UK market. Some businesses do not want deregulation because they believe that the regulations prevent sharp operators from taking advantage of customers. They prefer the guarantee of reputable service which the regulations give to the industry. It seems likely that private providers of care in the community for the old and disabled will require more regulation rather than less.

3 Legislation on monopoly and competition

Monopoly

Control over industry is necessary to prevent the excesses of a market in which companies use their power with insufficient consideration for the consumer or the effects on small businesses. A business with a monopoly can restrict output in order to be able to charge a higher price. This will enable it to earn higher profits but the consumer gets a smaller quantity at a higher price and is clearly worse off. An inefficient allocation of resources is the result.

Competition policy is built on a theoretical framework which has four elements:

1 determinants
2 structure
3 conduct
4 performance.

The 'determinants' of the industry might be price elasticity of demand for the product, economies of scale and vertical integration. These will explain the 'structure' of the industry, which is defined by the market share of companies, barriers to entry and concentration ratios. Once the structure of the industry is understood, it is possible to predict how businesses behave (their 'conduct', be it collusion or competition) and, consequently, what their 'performance' will be (defined in terms of profit levels and prices).

This theoretical framework does not explain everything within a market. There are many times when the model breaks down, e.g. when a very successful company, making high profits, is able to reduce its prices and drive other businesses into bankruptcy. In this case the company's performance is controlling the structure of the industry. In general, however, this view of industrial organisation can be helpful in analysing many market situations.

A variety of techniques is available to the government in its attempts to control markets. The most recent legislation that allows businesses to be investigated is the **Competition Act 1980**. Its basic starting point concerns the practice of individual companies and whether these activities are anti-competitive. The procedure in these situations is that the Director-General of Fair Trading is required to investigate alleged anti-competitive practices. Where such practices exist, the Director-General can order them to be stopped or the whole matter can be referred to the Monopoly and Mergers Commission. This organisation then considers the case and publishes its recommendations. The final decision is taken by the relevant secretary of state, on the basis of whether it is in the 'public interest'. This test of acceptability means that, in the view of the Department of Trade and Industry (DTI), on balance, the benefits of the activity to the public outweigh the costs, taking into consideration both the current and future position. Figure 5.1 summarises this process.

Figure 5.1 UK monopoly legislation

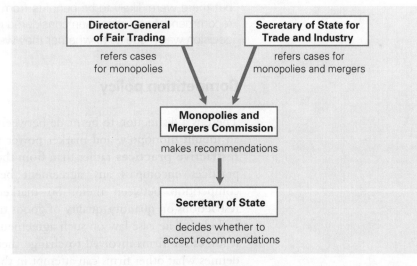

British Gas

Following the privatisation of British Gas (BG) in 1986, there have been a number of investigations into the amount of competition within the industry. British Gas has a monopoly over the supply of gas to domestic users as well as control over the supply to industrial customers. The first enquiry by the Monopolies and Mergers Commission (MMC) was in 1988, which called for greater competition in the supply of commercial customers. In 1991 the Office of Fair Trading (OFT) looked at whether British Gas had complied with this request by the MMC and concluded that it had not. OFT demanded that British Gas sell some of its contracts and split the transmission of gas from the rest of its business in order to increase competition from new entrants. In 1992 British Gas undertook to give up 60% of the market to supply industrial customers by 1995 and to create accounts for the transport and storage of gas so that no other supplier would face discriminatory prices for the use of pipelines. Later in 1992, the MMC was asked to investigate whether British Gas's pipeline monopoly was in the public interest. There was, at the same time, another reference to the MMC, to look at the determination of domestic prices.

The recommendations in August 1993 included the following:

1 BG should be split into two companies: one involving the selling of gas, the other involving the maintenance and sale of appliances.
2 The monopoly for domestic supplies should be reduced in size to users of 1,500 therms or less per year (from 2,500).

3 BG should be allowed to earn a return of 6.5% to 7.5% on new investments.

The report argued that the monopoly was not against the public interest but there were 'likely to be benefits from allowing competition'. These recommendations were then considered by the government before the decision was made as to whether they were implemented.

Competition policy

There is a distinction to be made between market power where there is an inbuilt monopoly, and market power which results from the use of **restrictive practices** rather than from the market structure. Restrictive practices encompass any agreement between firms which reduces competition between them. So market sharing, price agreements, restrictions on quantity, quality of goods traded or on distribution are all included. The case law on such agreements is important, partly because it forces the firms involved to change their ways, but mainly because it defines what other firms can attempt in the future. Once it is established that a certain practice is illegal, for the most part the practice will not be used. Figure 5.2 shows how restrictive practices are investigated.

Figure 5.2 UK restrictive practices legislation

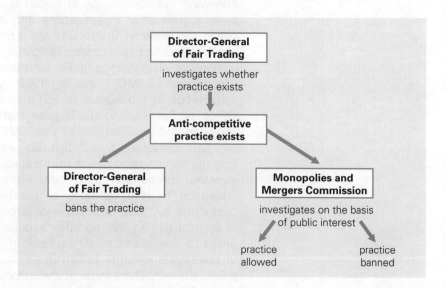

Referrals to the Monopolies and Mergers Commission

Recent cases referred to the MMC include ice cream, bus companies and perfume. The MMC does not always find against the firm which has been referred to it. In the case of perfumes, the producers were allowed to carry on restricting distribution in order to preserve the luxury image of the product.

The word from OFT

Competition is an essential element in the efficient working of markets. It encourages enterprise, productivity and choice. In doing so it enables consumers to buy the goods they want at the best possible price. By encouraging efficiency in industry, competition in the domestic market also contributes to our international competitiveness.

The overall aim of UK competition policy is to encourage and enhance the competitive process. When the process is adversely affected, the law provides a number of ways in which the situation can be examined and, if necessary, altered.

Competition is not regarded as an end in itself. With some exceptions, there is no assumption that a particular type of action or a particular situation which reduces competition is wrong in itself. The legislation provides for case by case examinations and only when a matter is found to be, or likely to be, against the public interest can it be prohibited.

Source: Office of Fair Trading, 1990

The EU and competition policy

The majority of European Union legislation concerning competition is covered in two Articles that have been in force since the signing of the Treaty of Rome. A unified approach to competition policy is an important objective for the EU, so that all firms may face competitive markets across all member countries.

Article 85 of the Treaty of Rome attempts to prevent restrictive practices, such as price fixing or market sharing agreements, which affect trade between member countries. The existence of these can be hard to prove. The following case study shows how one offender was treated.

The EU and British Steel

BRITISH Steel was yesterday fined £24.3 million for breaking European rules outlawing price fixing. Sixteen leading steel makers were found guilty of operating a cartel to supply the construction industry. The penalties were accompanied by a stiff warning that the Commission would take a tough line against market-rigging.

The Commission's decision was bitterly criticised during angry exchanges in the House of Commons. MPs of all parties said the judgement was unfair to British Steel. However, in its leader, the FT suggested that although the steel industry was in a mess, a market solution might prove better than a cartel.

Source: *Financial Times*, 17 February 1994

Article 86 of the Treaty of Rome attempts to deal with the abuse of a dominant position within a market. The concept of market dominance is not only defined according to the share of the market and the size of the company; other factors, such as the range of products, can be considered too. The regulations prohibit limiting production and imposing prices, among other monopolistic practices. The following case studies indicate the scope of EU action on monopolies.

Hoffman-la Roche v Commission 1979

The multinational pharmaceutical company Hoffman-la Roche entered into exclusive supply contracts with industrial purchasers. These contracts contained 'fidelity rebates', which ensured that moneys were returned if certain sales targets were met. The European Court decided that this was an abuse of the company's dominant position and the practice had 'the effect of hindering the maintenance of the degree of competition still existing in the market or the growth of that competition'.

The EU and *Radio Times*

Radio Times has the largest circulation of all magazines in the UK. This position has been built up because of its monopoly control over the information it contains. Traditionally, the magazine has been the only source of television and radio listings up to one week before the programmes are shown. Similarly, *TV Times* used to hold control over the listings of the commercial television programmes. This monopoly power has been challenged in both the UK and EU courts.

The first challenge to their monopoly positions came in 1983 when *Time Out* published advance notice of television programmes. The UK courts granted an injunction to prevent distribution of the magazine, thereby confirming the monopoly rights held by the BBC and ITV publishers. In 1985 an established publisher in Ireland started printing advance notice of television programmes for the whole of Ireland. The BBC and ITV publishers sought an injunction, but the Irish publishers brought a case to the EU courts on the grounds of abuse of a monopoly position under Article 86 of the Treaty of Rome. In 1989 the court took the view that the arrangements were restrictive and did prevent competition. In addition the court ruled that the BBC and ITV publishers should make the information available to other publishers via a licensing agreement with reasonable royalties.

After some delay, there is now a variety of competing publications which list the whole week's viewing in one magazine.

Open Question

Is competition policy effective?

It is in the nature of things that we do not know how many restrictive practices go unnoticed by the authorities. It is possible that, despite regulations in both the UK and Brussels, there is still a great deal of collusion going on.

4 Other means of control

Self-regulatory bodies

Traditionally, some parts of UK business, especially in the financial services sector, have regulated themselves. In recent years they have been brought under the wing of the Securities and Investments Board which was set up under the 1986 Financial Services Act. These businesses are not controlled directly by legislation but follow a self-imposed code of practice. These self-regulatory bodies have persuaded the government that they can do a better job of 'policing' their own practitioners than the legal framework could. Under the Act, they can only continue to be self-regulated if it can be shown that this is in the consumers' interests.

LAUTRO

LAUTRO regulates life assurance and unit trust companies. The organisation lays down rules about how investments can be sold to the general public. These rules cover advertising material, salespeople's visits, telephone calls, sales letters, etc. Most life insurance and unit trust members belong to LAUTRO and they must adopt its rules if they wish to continue selling their products to the public. Their regulations are intended to protect the public from being given wrong or biased advice. This arrangement can be more flexible than legislation, but it can also operate in the interests of the business rather than the consumer.

The personal pensions scandal, outlined in the case study on p. 105, comes within the remit of LAUTRO and of FIMBRA, the self-regulatory body for independent financial advisers. If, in fact, these bodies had been operating as intended, people could not have been given misleading financial advice. As it was, sales personnel appear to have ignored the regulatory rules altogether. There is also a possibility that some sales people have offered money in exchange for introductions to potential clients – a serious breach of the rules.

The regulators did not uncover the failure of the industry to comply with the standards demanded for a very long time. The requirements appear to have been completely ineffective. The only faintly plausible excuse on offer is that some sales of pension plans were made while the rules were still being devised.

Open Question

Is self-regulation effective?

These events raise serious questions about the effectiveness of self-regulation. Many in the financial services sector would prefer to see effective government regulation put in place.

Other kinds of self-regulation

Some regulatory activities take place entirely independently of the government. There are currently 53 different arbitration schemes, organised by the Chartered Institution of Arbitrators, which aim to look after consumers' interests. Consumers who feel an organisation has not met its side of the contract can seek arbitration (if there is a scheme in the relevant area) which is final and legally binding on both parties. The advantages of using this sort of scheme, rather than going to court, are that it is cheap and user-friendly and legal representatives are not needed.

Professional associations, such as the British Medical Association, also play a role in ensuring that standards are maintained in the provision of services.

Other independent organisations include the Advertising Standards Authority, a voluntary organisation which, in theory, ensures that all advertisments are 'legal, decent, honest and truthful'. In practice, it exerts only limited control over the industry.

Linking the private and public sectors

The London Underground

The London Underground was built and then run by the public sector. The costs of construction were met by the taxpayer. In 1988 the Transport Secretary announced the extension of one of the tube lines, which would run from central London to Docklands. This extension of the Jubilee Line would be financed jointly by private sector and public sector funds. This was approved by Parliament in 1989 and a private construction firm committed £400 million to the overall cost of £1 billion (the remaining £600 million would be paid by the government). The final contracts were signed in October 1993 and passengers are expected to use the service in April 1998.

By providing part of the funding, the government achieves a degree of control over the decisions made. Equally, it can be sure that the operation will run on commercial lines because the private sector would not participate otherwise.

A basic principle of the market economy is that those who benefit from a project should pay for it. Matching the benefits to the costs will allow the government to get better value for taxpayers' money as it will be able to seek assistance from other interested parties. This approach has been seen in many smaller-scale building projects, particularly in the creation of out-of-town shopping centres where the retail outlets have often paid for new roads to be constructed. If the private sector can be persuaded of the advantage of a project then governments can expect a contribution to the costs. This is known as planning gain.

Taxes and subsidies

Tax incidence

Governments can exert control over markets by using their power to tax or by providing subsidies for certain activities. The range of products which are taxed over and above the standard VAT rate gives plenty of clues as to governments' motives. Taxes are used to raise revenue but this is only part of the story. Taxes on tobacco discourage smoking; taxes on fossil fuels discourage the environmental degradation that occurs when they are burned. Subsidies paid to farmers in environmentally sensitive areas reduce the damage done by modern farming techniques.

Import controls

Import duties have a different effect. By protecting domestic producers, they often give them more market power, reducing competition from abroad. Consumers' positions are thus weakened; they pay a higher price and may well have less choice.

5 The power of the European Union

The European Economic Community (EEC), now known as the European Union, began in 1957 with the signing of the Treaty of Rome. The original six members (Germany, France, The Netherlands, Belgium, Luxembourg and Italy) were joined by Ireland, Denmark and the UK in 1973 and later by Spain, Portugal and Greece. The member countries agree to the basic principle that, within the EU, businesses compete with each other on an equal basis. Norway, Sweden, Finland and Austria are expected to be the next to join.

EU competition policy has already been described. In addition to the two main Articles, there are other ways in which the EU can influence the level of competition within any national economy. It has been involved in negotiations with the rest of the world via the GATT talks, aiming to reduce the level of tariffs throughout the world. Reducing import controls encourages competition and limits any one firm's market power.

Excess supply

The latest set of trade negotiations also considered the EU's Common Agricultural Policy. This has often been seen to disadvantage the consumer and world producers in order to benefit farmers, so the effect is rather the opposite of EU industrial policy.

Common Agricultural Policy

Since the start of the EEC, now the European Union, it has always been the policy to ensure that farmers receive a common price for agricultural products throughout the member states. All agricultural produce is priced in ECUs and converted to domestic prices via the current exchange rate. The system works through intervention in the market place to ensure that the farmers receive a guaranteed minimum price. When market forces are such that the equilibrium price is above the minimum, there is no need for the EU to intervene. If, however, the market-determined equilibrium price is below the guaranteed minimum (as it usually is), the EU will increase the demand and buy up produce, forcing the price to rise. In doing this the EU will end up with surplus produce that it does not want. (These are the legendary butter mountains and wine lakes.) This produce is then sold outside the EU so as not to influence the internal price.

Figure 5.3 shows a guaranteed price above the free market equilibrium price and the excess supply which results.

Figure 5.3

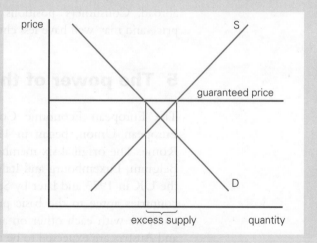

The emerging Central European states

Several Central European countries are interested in joining the European Union as they wish to gain access to the large Western markets. At present, the EU is granting *preferred trading status* to some of the newly developing market economies but this may not be enough to satisfy the aspirations of many of the Central European governments.

The example of Poland

Negotiations between Poland and the EU started in 1990 and an agreement was signed in December 1991, granting Poland membership of a free trade area. This would allow the removal of internal barriers between Poland and the EU but leave each country free to establish its own external barriers to trade. This agreement has been ratified by the Polish government but, before it can come into effect, it must be accepted by the parliaments of all the EU member countries. This has not yet happened.

Until this happens, there is an interim agreement which allows limited free trade. In reality, this only affects industrial products and not agricultural goods. By the beginning of March 1992, the EU had removed 54% of all its barriers to trade with Poland. The full removal of barriers to trade will take another ten years. As well as removing some of the trade barriers the 1991 agreement allowed:

- EU-based businesses to invest in Poland on a non-discriminatory basis
- agreements on education and scientific transfer.

It did not allow for the free migration of workers from Poland to the EU nor the end of export tariffs on agricultural products, where Poland has considerable cost advantages.

It is hard to say what effect the expansion of the EU might have on market power. To the extent that competition might well increase, many firms might find their market power threatened.

Other European provision

The European Single Market Act, which came into force in the UK on 1 January 1993, created a single trading area within the European Union. The consequences of this legislation are far reaching and some of the main effects on businesses are:

- There are no official internal barriers to trade within the EU.
- There are no restrictions on the internal movement of labour or capital within the EU.
- If a product can be sold in one EU country, then it can be sold in all EU countries.
- Any subsidy given by a government to an industry can be investigated by the EU to see if it gives an unfair advantage to one country's industry.

It is expected that these measures will increase competition within the EU.

Open Question

What is the likely overall
effect of the single market
on the market power of
business generally?

European Health and Safety at Work directives came into force at the beginning of January 1993. These requirements replace the UK's own law, the Health and Safety at Work Act 1974. These new regulations place a duty or responsibility upon employers to protect:

- their employees
- other people, including members of the public, who may be affected by work being done.

Self-employed people also have duties under these regulations to protect themselves and other people. In many ways these directives are a good example of how the EU operates. They replace out-of-date laws in individual countries with new regulations that create standardised European practices.

Some EU provision runs counter to the aim of deregulating. EU controls do, however, attempt to create a 'level playing-field' for competing firms. To the extent that member countries comply with the rules, this encourages competition and increases consumer choice, probably reducing firms' market power to some degree.

Market power and governments

The general thrust of government competition policy is to try to reduce market imperfections, which can distort the prices facing consumers. However, governments create their own distortions. Regulation has the effect of introducing constraints upon the market. Because of the many and various market imperfections, each market situation is individual and unique and must be evaluated as such.

Whether a business or an individual has some power in the market place depends upon a whole range of considerations relating to the particular circumstances of the situation. It should also be kept in mind that some firms dominate their market, yet seek to act in the interests of the consumer. Meantime, in other markets anti-competitive practices may go on unnoticed for a long time. However, the degree of market power can change rapidly as new entrants come into the market, as technology changes or as the pattern of comparative advantage shifts.

Businesses often feel that employee-protection laws and competition policies tie their hands, preventing them from performing as well as they might. In reality many highly successful businesses face very strong competition indeed. The competition acts as a spur to excellence. Once achieved, the capacity to compete effectively opens, rather than closes, doors.

Index